WHAT EVERY GIRL SHOULD KNOW

This book is brilliant! I wish I'd had it!
Katie Bull (Dr. Dave's sister)

This book is dedicated to all the people who have helped me in my career – from my medical colleagues to friends and co-workers in television and the media, particularly everyone at BBC Children's Factual Programmes, and BBC Newsround, without whom this book would not have been possible.

Special thanks to Hilary, my agent, for keeping me sane.

Dr. David Bull MB, BS, Bsc, ASM
Dr. David Bull lives and works in London. As well as being a medical practitioner, he is an award-winning presenter of television and radio programs about medical and social issues of special importance to teenagers.

Also by the same author:
COOL AND CELIBATE? SEX OR NO SEX

WHAT EVERY GIRL SHOULD KNOW

The ultimate A-Z guide to health
and emotional concerns for
girls and young women

Dr. DAVID BULL

Edited by Helen Wire

ELEMENT
CHILDREN'S BOOKS

SHAFTESBURY, DORSET · BOSTON, MASSACHUSETTS · MELBOURNE, VICTORIA

© Element Children's Books 1999
Text © Dr. David Bull 1999

First published in Great Britain in 1999 by
Element Children's Books
Shaftesbury, Dorset SP7 8BP

Published in the USA in 1999 by
Element Books, Inc.
160 North Washington Street,
Boston MA 02114

Published in Australia in 1999 by
Element Books and distributed by
Penguin Australia Limited,
487 Maroondah Highway, Ringwood,
Victoria 3134

Cover design by Zoom Design.
Typeset by Dorchester Typesetting Group Ltd.
Printed and bound in Great Britain by Creative Print and Design (Wales) Ebbw Vale

British Library Cataloguing in Publication data available.
Library of Congress Cataloging in Publication data available.

ISBN 1 902618 18 1

CONTENTS

INTRODUCTION

Hi, I'm Doctor David Bull. How, you may ask, do I – a man – know *what every girl should know*? Well, of course I don't know everything but I can certainly help you understand a lot about how your body works and how much better life can be if you keep it fit and healthy. And I can also give you a few tips about those inner feelings we all have – even some from a boy's point of view.

From the enthusiastic response I get from teenagers and children whenever I present a program on television, I do know how much girls *want* to know. So, I've gathered together in this book as much information, help, and advice as I can possibly cram into it. Every entry could easily be the subject of a whole book but I've tried to give you a clear overview and understanding of some vital issues as well as suggesting where else you may to find out more or get help.

A lot of what is in this book may seem horribly scary but nothing can be scarier than *not knowing* what's happening to you if something goes wrong. Most of the medical problems will only happen to other people but I hope this book will help you help yourself as well as enabling you to be sensitive to any of your friends who seem to be in trouble. Another essential thing this book tries to do is to tell you how health problems may be prevented before they start and how to deal with them if they do.

One important thing I learned as a teenager was never to be embarrassed about *not knowing* something, or about asking for help. We are not born with all the knowledge of the world programed into our brains; we learn it bit by bit. Sometimes it comes to us in brilliant flashes of understanding; at others through a long accumulation of information and experience, or a combination of the two. As far as I am concerned:

KNOWLEDGE IS POWER!
If you don't know something, ask someone who does.

Often your parents know more than you think, or you can try older relations, friends, teachers, your family doctor, sports coach, etc. Whatever your problem, fear, or longing, you won't be the only one who has felt that way and you won't be the last. There's bound to be someone who can help you or tell you where to get help. The right person is different for all of us and who it is will depend on what you want to know or what help you need. Book stores, libraries, the Internet, local telephone directories, and support groups are all mines of information. Try them all, till you get what you need.

The better informed you are about anything, the better and faster you will be able to decide what to do about it. As a teenager you are racing toward your own independence and as you start making your own decisions you will realize it can be very scary but also how it feels great to be taking control. Every choice you make will affect the whole course of your life and no one person could possibly tell you everything you'll need to know along the way. But I hope you find in this book a good deal of *what every girl should know.*

Good luck and have fun!

Dr. David Bull

Does an apple a day keep the doctor away?

To be healthy, eat fruit every day. It helps arm your body to fight infections, keep your bowel functioning normally and to protect you from heart disease and cancers. Wash fruit and dry it well. Lots of unwashed germy hands may have touched it before you sink your teeth into its lusciousness.

ABILITY

We are all born with the potential for excelling in different ways. Some girls have the kind of physique that makes them great sportswomen while others have a special talent for such things as music, drawing, teaching, or caring for people. But a lot of us are just reasonably good at a number of things and it takes time to sift out what we *don't* want to do and find what really interests and fulfils us. As opportunities and choices present themselves try to tackle them all with enthusiasm and they are almost bound to offer up something that will interest you and help you decide what to try next or what to aim for.

See also **Assertiveness**, **Choices**, **Decisions**, **Education**, **Opportunity**, **Independence**, **You**.

ABUSE

Sadly, this is something we often hear about in the media. Almost all forms of abuse involve a strong person picking on someone younger or weaker. Children therefore are vulnerable to abuse from some adults.

Most adults are loving and protective of the children in their care. But sometimes things go wrong and a girl can find herself living in fear of someone she should have been able to trust. If this is happening to you, get help. *No one* has the right to harm you or to force you to do anything you feel is wrong.

Any kind of abuse is a misuse of personal power. It is wrong and there should be no place for it in society. It can range from mild to severe and can make you miserable, so if it's happening to you *now* is the time to put a stop to it. The most common forms are verbal or emotional, physical and sexual abuse, and neglect. Sometimes, abuse can include a combination of these.

Verbal or emotional abuse *is when you are constantly called horrible names, insulted, threatened, or made to feel negative about yourself or your abilities by what is said to you.*

The old saying, *sticks and stones may break my bones but words will never hurt me,* is good advice but it is not always easy to simply ignore verbal bullies. Consistent verbal insults and threats *do* hurt and in extreme cases can cause lasting psychological damage.

Bullying like this is common but most schools are now trying to stamp it out. The advice from children who have been bullied is always the same: *you must tell someone you trust and get help as soon as possible.* Don't allow bullying to continue in the hope that the bullies will get bored and stop. Tell a best friend, a teacher, a parent, or check out your local phone directory and phone a

Linda was Bullied

Linda, aged 12, was constantly called names at school. She was picked on by a group of older and stronger girls. The bullying got so bad that she had to leave school temporarily and have lessons at home. Not content with what they had done, the girls stood outside her house chanting vile insults.

Linda's parents spoke to the Principal of the school who discussed the problem with the bullies and their parents, making it clear the girls would be expelled if they ever bullied anyone again. She also organized class discussions about bullying and self-assertiveness, and set up a Bully Box in which pupils could put an anonymous note to report any instances of bullying. As a result, the culprits were dealt with immediately and bullying was brought under control within the school.

child helpline. Any serious threats or violence to yourself and your family should be reported to the police. Never give up. Keep telling people until you find someone who really does help you. Until then, try to avoid being on your own where the bullies can get at you; and try always to do things with a group of friends.

**If you're being bullied
never suffer in silence.
TELL A RESPONSIBLE ADULT.**

Physical abuse is when you are beaten up, hit, kicked, excessively punished or hurt in any physical way by anyone more powerful than you are.

Although physical abuse does happen in schools, it's even worse if it happens at home. Sadly, some children are physically battered by a parent, a step-parent, or some other relative. Often, they are told to keep quiet or they will be hit again. The only way out of this dreadful situation is to get professional help. Tell an adult you trust, maybe your mother, father, aunt, teacher, or doctor, or look in the phone directory for a confidential child helpline to call for advice.

See also **Alcohol**.

Sexual abuse is when you are used for sex against your will. No adult should touch the private parts of your body unless there's a good reason and you are happy about it. In most countries it is illegal for an adult male to have sexual intercourse with young girls under 16. In some countries a girl has to be 17, 18, or 21, depending on which country or state they live in.

Sexual abuse is vile and should never happen. It's mostly done in secret and is forced on a young person usually by someone older. Often, it is someone they know and should be able to trust. **It is never the child's fault**. Sexually abused girls are told things like, *Don't tell anyone. It's our little secret;* or, *If you tell anyone you'll be put in a children's home and never see your mother again,* or the abuser threatens to hurt the girl or someone she cares about if she doesn't do what he (or sometimes she) wants.

The only way to break the cycle is to tell a responsible adult who you know you can trust, or to phone a confidential child helpline. Don't suffer in silence hoping it will stop – it won't until you get someone to protect you from it.

If anyone tries to touch you in a way you don't want, say, *No, I don't want you to do that. I will tell the police (or the Principal, my father/mother/brother) unless you leave me alone, now.* Run home, to a friend's house, to your teacher, to your doctor's office, anywhere you know you will be safe.

Of course, you will hug and play physical games with adults who are close to you, and this is great and perfectly natural and innocent. But you will know the difference when someone is touching you in the wrong way and telling you to keep it secret. Don't let them.

Neglect *is when the adults who should be responsible for your well-being do not protect, feed, and support you adequately.*

EVERY GIRL HAS THE RIGHT TO BE LOVED, PROTECTED, AND WELL CARED FOR AND TO RECEIVE A GOOD EDUCATION.

You should have enough food to eat, warm clothes, and a safe place to live. You are neglected if you don't get enough food to eat, are unable to wash, or have nowhere safe to sleep. It is also neglect if a parent or carer knows a girl is being abused in any way and does not protect her or report the abuser to the appropriate authorities. And maybe the person who is failing to protect you has been forced into a situation where they can't, and they will need help too.

Where to Get Help

If you need help, you are not alone. Every day, thousands of children seek help from their parents, teacher, librarian, doctor, social services department, police, or support groups set up especially to help young people. There are hundreds of good people waiting to help you, so never be shy about asking, and persist until you get the help and support you need.

Any young person in danger, distress, or with any problem can call a child helpline for free confidential help and advice. See **Support Groups** at the end of this book.

ACNE

There are few things more certain than that spots (pimples, zits) will erupt on your face the very day you are to appear in the school play, or you have a date with your dream boy.

Spots are revolting. They don't appear in some inconspicuous place (like between your toes), but erupt on the most visible part of you – your face and sometimes your shoulders – making you look as if you have some ghastly contagious disease. No one could blame you for thinking spots will ruin your life. They won't.

OK, here's the good news. Spots are common. You would be an extraordinary teenager if you *didn't* have them. Most people do grow out of them but it can take years. What you need to know is that *you can do something about them.*

There are three types of spot:

- **papules** (red),
- **pustules** (white),
- **blackheads**.

What Causes Spots?

Tiny pores lead to the sweat and sebaceous glands in our skin. During puberty, a child's body grows into its adult shape. The extra hormonal activity involved in this burst of growth causes glands in your skin to produce an excess of sebum (natural oil) which makes the skin greasy. Bacteria love this and start to grow in it. As they break down the fatty sebum a blackhead is formed.

The black substance isn't dirt, it's the skin pigment *melanin*. The blackhead blocks the pore duct and will stay there until it is either *eased* out or it becomes inflamed. When both the duct and the gland become inflamed a whitehead appears. Eventually, this bursts and the healing process begins.

Things You Should Know

❥ Acne can start when you are as young as 8-9 years of age and peaks between the ages of 14-18.

❥ Acne is often worse just before a period.

❥ Acne is *not* contagious. You can't catch it from or give it to anyone else.

❥ Eating chocolate does not cause spots, but eating lots of fresh fruit and vegetables, and drinking water, will help your body work efficiently and you'll feel and look better.

❥ Stress can make spots worse. See **Relaxation**.

❥ Constant rubbing against the skin by such things as a headband or a bag strap can cause spots.

❥ Cheap make-up can cause spots.

❥ If you wear make-up, choose a light non-greasy one and be sure to wash it off *every* night before going to bed.

❥ Wash your hair regularly and wear it back off your forehead.

❥ Sunlight may improve your spots but overexposure is dangerous. See **Suntan and Protection**.

❥ Sunbeds are not recommended.

Dr. Dave's Top Tips – Spots

There's no quick cure but at least you can make it harder for those spots to thrive. Work down this list until you find what works best for you.

Make cleansing a regular routine: And learn to love it; you may need to do it for years.

Wash every day: First, wash your face with warm water to open the pores. Then wash with an antibacterial cleansing solution in warm water. Rinse your face thoroughly and, finally, splash cold water over it to close the pores.

Use cleansing pads: These remove dead skin and sebum that has built up in the pores.

Use a cleansing solution, not soap: Soap dries out the skin which doesn't help. There are loads of specially formulated cleansing solutions on the market and most of them contain Benzoyl Peroxide. Always read and follow the instructions carefully. Start with the lowest concentration. Using more than the recommended amount will *not* clear up your spots any faster and may even harm your skin.

Removing blackheads: After washing, while your hands and face are still clean, gently stretch (not squeeze) the skin around each one and apply a little pressure with a blackhead remover (available and cheap from pharmacists).

Red, yellow, or green spots: Think of your spots as traffic lights. Red: Don't touch. Yellow: Gently stretch the skin around a spot to expel pus without damaging your skin.

Green!: It's infected. Go to your doctor.
Everyone does it but picking and squeezing spots can
spread bacteria and may cause permanent scarring.
Whenever you feel the urge, exert your willpower to stop
yourself, get away from the mirror, and quickly find
something more interesting to do – read a book, put on a
CD and have a dance. Eat an apple.

When To See The Doctor

If you don't see any improvement in 2-3 months it's time to see
your doctor. Ask a supportive adult to accompany you. Some
doctors will be helpful but others may give the impression they
think you're making an unnecessary fuss. Nonetheless, persist!

Only increase the concentration of your cleansing solution if
your doctor advises it. Antibiotics may be prescribed either to rub
on the skin or to take by mouth. Read and follow instructions
exactly. Some antibiotic treatments may make your skin sensitive
to sunlight. In serious cases, if antibiotics don't work, a drug to
reduce sebum production may be described. It may cause side
effects such as dryness of eyes, nose and lips.

SPOT CONTROL
Self-help, then get help.

Complementary Advice

➤ Every day, drink 6-8 glasses of water.
➤ Try washing with sandalwood or calendula soap.
➤ Teatree oil is naturally antibacterial. Mix one drop into five
   drops of organic olive oil and smooth this over your skin. If it
   stings, dilute with more olive oil.

ADDICTION

Being addicted to any substance (such as nicotine, drugs, or alcohol) means you really can't face a single day without having it. And that's not because it makes you feel good, but because you feel absolutely awful if you don't have it. An addict desperately needs to have what they are addicted to – just to feel normal!

An addiction to any substance is said to be *psychological* if you can't cope with your everyday life without first having some; or *physical* if you experience horrendous symptoms if you don't have it. Withdrawal from drugs such as heroin is both agonizing and terrifying.

Almost always, addictions lead to other problems, such as: lying to parents, losing friends, stealing to pay for drugs, not being able to concentrate at school, being expelled, becoming homeless, losing control of your life, physical and mental pain, and sometimes even early death.

Friends or older kids might offer you cigarettes or drugs and tease you if you don't want to take them. You might even be tempted to experiment. But don't! *Anyone* can become addicted – some more easily than others. The only way to ensure you're not one of them is *not* to take any drugs or cigarettes in the first place!

If you, or anyone you care about, has an addiction problem, *now* is the time to start conquering it. You'll need help, so try to speak calmly to your parents or carer, a teacher or doctor, and contact an appropriate support group.

See also **Alcohol, Assertiveness, Drugs, Smoking, Willpower,** and **Support Groups.**

AIDS (ACQUIRED IMMUNODEFICIENCY SYNDROME)

AIDS is an incurable condition caused by a virus known as HIV (human immunodeficiency virus). HIV destroys certain blood cells in the body and leaves the immune system unable to fight off infections. This means that when a person with AIDS catches an infection, their body can't fight it off as it would do normally. After contracting a number of illnesses, the person will almost certainly die of one of them.

AIDS is caught by having unprotected sex (i.e. without using a condom) with someone who carries the HIV in their body; or through absorption of HIV-infected blood. It can also be passed from a pregnant mother to her unborn child.

Millions of males *and females* have HIV and AIDS. Vital research is being done to find a cure but it has not yet been found. However, combination therapy drugs that have to be taken every day for as long as the person lives are at least giving people with AIDS longer to live.

See also **HIV** and **Sex**.

ALCOHOL

The odd thing about alcohol is that, unlike other *addictive* drugs, it is legal. However, it is illegal for anyone to sell it to young teenagers. The age when you can legally buy alcohol varies. In the UK, Europe, and Australia you have to be 18. In the USA you have to be 21.

Your first taste of alcohol may be in the form of alcopops a fruit drink designed to appeal to young people. They taste great and you might not realize they're alcoholic! But, alcopops can contain up to 20 percent by volume of alcohol. This is staggering (as you might be if you drink them) when compared to wine (11 percent) and beer (3-5 percent).

See also **Addiction**.

Why Alcohol Affects Children Badly

The liver breaks down alcohol into chemicals that can be eliminated from the body. Because a child's liver is not fully developed it has to struggle to do this job and even small quantities of alcohol can be very dangerous for them.

Alcohol is absorbed via the stomach lining into the bloodstream. After traveling around the body it crosses the blood-brain barrier and starts trouble!

Long-term Effects of Alcohol Abuse

BODY PARTS AFFECTED	ILL EFFECTS
BRAIN	Can cause fits and long term memory loss.
GUT	Ulcers. Swelling of the pancreas. Inflammation of the stomach lining. Can lead to hospitalization.
LIVER	Swelling of the liver (hepatitis); destruction of the liver (cirrhosis); and death.
HEART	Alcohol can cause a heart to miss beats. It increases blood pressure and can cause the heart to fail.
IMMUNE SYSTEM	Damage to the immune system leaves the body unable to fight off infections.
PREGNANCY	If a woman drinks alcohol during a pregnancy, her baby may be born deformed. Latest research shows drinking even small amounts during pregnancy may affect the development of the baby even after birth.
FAT	Alcohol makes you fat.

Alcohol Affects the Way We Function (Look at some of the adult behavior you see around you or on TV.)

While alcohol is in your body the coordination between your

senses and limbs is diminished. Moods change. At first, you may feel more relaxed, happy, less shy and more friendly, but alcohol also acts as a depressant and our negative feelings become exaggerated. Intoxication affects our eyesight; our reaction times slow down; and often we behave stupidly (although at the time it may seem funny). If you get very drunk you can lose your normal self-control and instincts for self-survival, and are more likely to behave in ways you could regret. You may wake the next day not only with an appalling headache but also with the deeply embarrassing knowledge that you have been kissing your best friend's boyfriend, or something even more serious!

Alcohol Causes Accidents

No one should ever drink and drive. Even the smallest amount of alcohol slows down our reaction times, making us more likely to cause an accident. Always refuse a lift with anyone who has been drinking. It's safer to walk (preferably with a *group* of friends if it's late), take a bus or taxi, or phone your parents to come and collect you. Even though they may grumble like crazy, there's not many parents who wouldn't rather get out of bed at night than lose you altogether!

**Never accept a lift from someone
who has been drinking alcohol.**

Grooving around to cool dance music, and being in with a crowd is fantastic. Nothing can match it – and you won't need alcohol to have a great time. But you will get thirsty, so drink plenty of water. It's a lot cheaper, too.

Some Parents are Violent

Children of drunken parents need help. And so does the parent who has a drinking problem. Alcohol affects some people very badly and makes them aggressive, even toward the people they love. A drunken irrational parent is both terrifying and deeply frustrating because it seems as if nothing you can do or say will calm them down. You can't defend yourself against the horrible things they shout at you because whatever you say or do only seems to infuriate them more and they may even get violent.

**Every child should feel and be safe from
harm in their own home.**

Unfairly, all the horror of a drunken parent can make a girl feel very bad and uncertain about herself. Don't! *It's not your fault.* Remember it is the parent who has a drinking problem and who needs help. If they are not willing to talk about what's happening and get professional help then the rest of the family should take steps either to leave the drunken parent or get a court order to keep him or her out of the family home. Although he or she has a drinking problem your parent probably really loves you and you love them and will want to see one another. This can be arranged in controlled circumstances so you won't feel in any danger.

Where to Get Help

If what is happening is really bad, get to a phone, call an emergency number and ask for the police. Tell them clearly what is happening and say you (and your family) need protection. Be ready to give them your name, address and phone number. The police should come to help you. They can also usually tell you if there is a refuge for women and children nearby where you can stay safely until another place to live is sorted out. If you or any member of your family has been beaten up, go to see a doctor as soon as possible. Apart from treating you, they will record the assault and this can be used as evidence if you need to get a court order to protect you from the beater. Ask the doctor to tell you where else you can get help. Look in the local phone book for alcohol helplines to call for confidential advice about what to do and where to get help for yourself, your parent, or your carer.

See **Support Groups** at the end of this book.

ALLERGIES

I can't eat that,
I'm allergic to it.

Having an allergy may seem like a great excuse for not eating school food, but allergies can be very serious. People have been known to die of bad reactions to foods as commonplace as eggs or peanuts.

Anyone who has an *allergy* to a particular substance is so hypersensitive to it that their body overreacts to its presence. Some common allergies are caused by dust-mite droppings; grass; pollen; metals such as the nickel in jewelry, especially if, like earrings, it pierces the body; bee stings; some foods; the cocktail of chemicals used around the home or school for cleaning, fire-proofing, and pest control; car emissions; some drugs such as antibiotics.

Allergic symptoms include: streaming or itchy nose and eyes, wheezing, fainting, skin rashes, coughing, abdominal pain, diarrhea.

Food Allergy

In a worst case scenario, a person who is allergic to peanuts could die if they ate even a tiny amount. For them, eating a peanut could set off the following chain reaction. When the mast cells, which line the lungs and the blood vessels, sense nuts in the body they release a number of chemicals into the blood including *histamine*. Breathing becomes difficult and the person starts to wheeze. Tissues such as the eyelids and lips start swelling; and a nasty rash might appear over the whole body. Severe swelling can block the throat and prevent the person from breathing.

Anyone with a food allergy should avoid the food. If you are allergic to peanuts, for example, you mustn't eat the slightest trace of one. Unfortunately, many foods including shop-bought biscuits, cakes, cereals and general foods often include traces of peanuts. You'd think it would be easy to avoid them by looking at the ingredients list on a label but trace amounts are not always listed. Did you know a ready-made lemon meringue pie may contain nuts? Neither did I!

**If you cook your own food
you'll know what's gone into it.**

Allergy to Metals

Some girls who wear cheap earrings become allergic to metals such as nickel and chromium and find they can only wear silver, gold, or surgical steel jewelry. The metal bits on bra straps can cause the skin to become inflamed and it may weep and crust. The only treatment is to remove the offending metal and avoid it in future.

Testing for Allergies

Soon after eating a particular food you may notice a mild allergic reaction. Chocolate or cheese, for example, may make you feel suddenly hot. Simply avoid the food and you'll be fine. But sometimes the cause is difficult to trace and you will need professional help to identify it. Your doctor may prescribe drugs such as anti-histamines. Ask to be referred to an allergy specialist or find a complementary practitioner who specializes in testing for allergies.

There are plenty of good books about allergies. If you think you may have an allergy, find out as much as you can about allergies so that you know how to avoid or control it.

See **Support Groups** at the end of this book.

AMBITION

Belief creates reality has always been one of my favorite maxims for life. No! I'm not mad, crazy, or bonkers. If you really want something, if you *really* believe what you want is right for you, and you work very hard at it, then I expect you *can* achieve almost anything. There may be a few setbacks along the way, but there's always something to be learned from them before you pick yourself up and start again. If you refuse to give up, you'll eventually get what you want.

At times you may feel frustrated, dejected, and rejected – all that's perfectly normal and will soon pass. Then it's up to you to choose your next step. Look at all your options, then make a decision about what to do. You could just give up and get pushed around, doing what other people want you to; or you can take control of your life and have another go. Or find something even more interesting to do. It's a bit like throwing mud at a wall. You have to keep doing it until some eventually sticks. And the more you throw, the more chance you have of some of it sticking!

Personally, I'm a bit of a fatalist. I think if you don't get picked for the team, or whatever, then it probably wasn't meant to be and something more exciting and more right for you will come along. This may or may not be true but it certainly makes it easier to deal with rejection.

Girls have never had so many opportunities to fulfil their potential but the competition can be fierce, so you'll need the best possible education or training you can get. Set your goals, believe in your own abilities, and make it happen.

ANGER

We all feel angry sometimes, especially girls going through all the physical changes of puberty. Some girls feel especially tense just before a period and may unfairly snap and scream at their family. Apologize as soon as you can and hopefully they'll understand!

Dr. Dave's Top Tips – Anger

Anger is often directed at parents who don't seem to understand your point of view. Wait until everyone is calm then try to talk to them about some of the worries you and they have. Try to understand their point of view and find a way of making yours clear to them.

Write them a note if it makes it easier to say everything clearly. Or rage into a diary. Both of these will help you.

Try to avoid getting into a locked battle with parents.

Get away from an explosive situation until you've calmed down enough to think and talk calmly to one another.

Find a way to express your anger. Literally run it off.

Go rollerblading, for a walk or run, beat up your pillow, hit a ball against a wall – anything that doesn't harm anyone!

It's never too late to apologize for an ugly outburst that you subsequently realize was unfair or unjustified.

If your anger is overwhelming and totally out of control, talk about it with an adult you trust and respect, see your doctor, or call a child helpline for advice.

However, a girl who is being badly treated is of course right to feel angry. She needs to find a way to express it and to talk to an understanding adult who can help her resolve whatever is causing her anger.

A lot of young people's anger is due to frustration, often with themselves for not knowing what they want to do, or even knowing what they want but not doing it. Indecision is deeply frustrating, so make a list of your options, consider them, and make a decision. Any decision is better than no decision. Go in that direction for as long as it seems right. You can always change your mind later. Don't let yourself get stuck, dithering.

ANOREXIA NERVOSA
See **Eating Disorders.**

ANTIBIOTICS
Before antibiotics were widely used, millions of people died of even minor infections. Antibiotics are fantastic but they *can only be used to treat illnesses caused by bacteria NOT those caused by viruses.* Colds and the flu are caused by viruses which cannot be fought off by antibiotics. So, if you have a cold, don't expect a doctor to prescribe an antibiotic.

The bacteria that antibiotics fight aren't stupid. If *all* the bacteria are not killed off by a course of antibiotic, they can mutate and make themselves resistant to it in future. Since bacteria can mutate faster than we can invent antibiotics, we could end up with illnesses for which we have no antibiotic capable of defending us when we really need it. That is why antibiotics must only be used when absolutely necessary. And, if you start a course of them *you must finish it.* That will ensure *all* the bacteria are killed off and none are left to mutate.

Another good reason for not using antibiotics too often is that they wipe out a lot of good bacteria (that your body needs) along with the bad ones. So, try to take them only if your own immune system is really losing the battle against an infection.

ANTISOCIAL HABITS

Spitting: I loathe it. Spitting is my pet hate. It is gross, especially when sportsmen do it on TV. Spitting can spread diseases, especially a lung disease called tuberculosis (TB).

Spit is a mixture of *saliva* and *phlegm*. Saliva moistens food to make swallowing easier and contains enzymes that begin the digestive process. Phlegm is swept up the air passages by tiny little hairs called *cilia,* carrying with it unwanted dust and bacteria from the lung passages. Healthy phlegm is white, but green phlegm indicates a lung infection.

Every time you spit you could infect someone else with your germs. If you need to get rid of phlegm, spit it into a tissue and flush it down the toilet, or put it in a plastic bag and bin it.

Nose-picking: Picking your nose in public is never going to make you the most sought-after girl in school. Odd that, since boys seem to think it's hilarious to flick *their* nose-pickings all around the classroom. Your nose is not there just to look pretty, you know. Tiny hairs in it filter dust from the air. Chemicals in it destroy some infections, and its many glands and blood vessels warm and humidify the air you breathe.

You may sometimes need to pick debris from your nose but eating it isn't a great idea. Your body works hard to rid itself of dust, nasty toxins, and bacteria, so why stick them straight back into your mouth? Also, despite how often you wash, bacteria live on your hands and can infect you if you lick your fingers. The decision is yours!

Not Washing Your Hands: Our hands are amazing sources of infection. Something like 500 bugs live on them at any one time. Most are harmless but some can make us sick. So, always wash your hands after going to the toilet and before preparing or eating food.

Not washing your hands is a sure way to pass on infections to other people or yourself, especially with viral illnesses such as colds or the flu. Those bugs just sit around on your hands just waiting to leap from your fingers into your mouth!

Researchers analyzed peanuts that had been in a bowl on a table. They contained 15 different types of urine – which just shows how few people wash their hands as often as they should!

Biting Your Nails: This is another unattractive habit that won't help your cool intelligent image. And, when you go for a job or university interview, bitten fingernails may indicate to some people that you are a very nervous person perhaps with psychological problems that would make you unsuitable! See **Willpower** for a few hints about how to give up the habit.

ASSERTIVENESS – GIRL POWER

Being assertive comes naturally to some lucky girls. They never seem to doubt their right to be and to do whatever they want. They are sure of themselves, know what they want to do, are enthusiastic about it, and they make it happen. Almost certainly, they will succeed in whatever they choose to do. And if they don't, they will have enjoyed it along the way and will go on to find something else they really want to do. They are also experts at saying *no* to anything they *don't* want to do. Watch these girls and see what you can learn. But don't try to be just like them. Aim always to be more strongly yourself. If you can be proud and sure of who *you* are and what you are good at you'll find it much easier to be assertive.

Some of us have to work hard to get what we want, not to let

Dr. Dave's Top Tips – Assertiveness

Recognize and value your unique strengths and qualities and build on them.

Work out and decide what you want and never be shy about stating it clearly.

If you don't know something, don't be shy or embarrassed about it, just ask someone who does. It's much easier and far less confusing than pretending you do know.

Put yourself forward for things you want to do, even if you're nervous about it. Just say out loud, *I think I could do that,* or *I'd like to try that.* Then as you begin to do it, you will learn that you *can* do whatever it is you have set your mind on. If you need help, ask.

People admire assertiveness, such as that shown by a doctor managing a very ill patient; or a patient making it clear to a doctor that they want to be kept clearly informed about their treatment.

Being assertive is knowing what is right for you and stating it clearly; being happy with who you are and what you can do; and taking positive responsibility for yourself. And it's not always easy to get it right. It's a huge relief when people are clear and assertive about what they want but if you do it too aggressively, you could sound arrogant or bossy which can irritate people.

When you are sure of what you want, put yourself forward in a way that lets people see you are keen, without being nightmarishly pushy. Think about it and go for it!

anyone push us around, and to be able to say *no* to what we don't want without hurting or offending anyone. It's far less confusing for everyone if you can state clearly what you think or want. For example, if there's a documentary on TV about the fashion industry or the origin of the human race that you *really* want to see, don't let your friends talk you into going to a disco. Just say clearly what *you* want to do and do it. Amazingly, your friends will soon get used to you knowing what you want and learn to accept that you mean what you say.

If you appear to be uncertain about something, there will always be someone else who'll make the decision for you and you may find yourself doing something you don't want to do and resenting it.

ATHLETE'S FOOT
See **Fungal Infections**.

Who matures first, boys or girls?

Girls mature faster than boys. All through the teen years girls are thought to be better able to cope with the pressures of school. They also understand that exams are an important step to having an interesting career. Girls often seem to find it easier and more necessary to plan for their future. This may be one of the reasons why girls *do* better in exams at this age than boys.

BABY-SITTING

There isn't a set age when you can baby-sit but you should be old enough to realize the important responsibilities of the job, and not be frightened to be in a house on your own with little children to protect. Many people think you should be at least 14. And you should definitely like little children.

Responsibilities may include playing with the children, putting them to bed at the appropriate time, listening for them when they are asleep, and reassuring them if they wake frightened. That means not having the TV on too loud, and not inviting all your friends around for a party. And don't use the phone to chat to your friends all night. It will show up on the phone bill and you may be asked to pay for your calls. You must know where to contact the parents or some other adult help. In an emergency, your own parents or guardian should be available to support and advise you, at least on the phone.

When I started baby-sitting I felt really grown up. It can be great fun but it is also an incredibly responsible and adult job. You will have the life of a small child or children in your care alone. The children may be asleep when you arrive and you can read, study, or watch TV all night. Or you may need to keep them amused for a while before putting them to bed. Children can be quite manipulative and may be having such fun with you they'll want to extend their bed time. They will be happy and settle down if you give them your full attention and play or read books with them. Read them stories or look at picture books with them in bed as this is a good way to calm them down and give them something good to think about as they drift off to sleep.

Baby-sitting can be scary if you are left with a miserable sick child or if a child has an accident and you don't know where to contact the parents or emergency services. Your job will be easier and less stressful if you know the answers to everything on the following checklist before you baby-sit.

Before the Parents Leave Checklist

➤ What time do the children go to bed?
➤ What is their usual routine?
➤ Are there any special things you should know, for example, does a child have any allergies, need to take any medicine, or have nightmares, etc.?
➤ Where will the parents be?
➤ Is there a contact phone number?
➤ What time do they expect to be home? (Tell your parents when *you* expect to be home.)
➤ Is there a phone number for someone else to contact if you can't reach the parents?
➤ What is the doctor's phone number?
➤ What is the local emergency phone number?

Getting home: Make sure you have discussed this with the parents. Is a responsible and trustworthy adult going to take you home at the end of the night or will they get you a cab? Are your parents going to collect you? Young girls should *never* walk home alone at night even if it is only "just down the street."

BACK PROBLEMS

Many students suffer from some kind of back pain as a result of constantly carrying heavy schoolbags or from sitting on school furniture which is the wrong size. The skeleton relies on the spine or backbone to hold the body upright. The spine is a curved S-shape made up of 24 bones called vertebrae which are cushioned from one another by discs. When a heavy bag is slung over one shoulder it causes the spine to bend unnaturally to one side, putting stress on the bones, muscles, and joints, and this can cause back pain.

Old-fashioned sloping desks were better for the spine than modern tables because pupils sat up straight with both feet on the floor and didn't have to hunch over them to work. Hunching over a table to work turns the *S*-shape of the spine into a *C*-shape, putting a strain on the back. As we become used to sitting in a slumped-over position, we become lazy and adopt a bad posture.

Dr. Dave's Top Tips to Keep Your Back on the Right Track

Apart from helping you to avoid back pain, the following tips will help you feel positive about yourself and look great.

Think and stand tall as if your head is attached by a piece of string to the ceiling. If you do that your shoulders will fall back naturally. You'll look great and be surprised how much better you feel.

Don't slump your shoulders forward to disguise your newly emerging breasts. Remember, everyone else will be feeling just as shy about theirs as you are.

Sit up straight with your feet flat on the floor, your bottom pushed against the back of the chair, and relax your shoulders.

Carry a backpack rather than a shoulder bag. Wear it on both shoulders to spread the weight evenly.

Lift weights properly by bending your knees and keeping your back straight.

Warm up your muscles by doing some gentle stretching exercises before doing any vigorous sport.

BAD BREATH

I used to have a teacher with bad breath. Every time she came near me I almost fainted! Sound familiar? Its medical name is halitosis and it is said to affect 25 percent of adults persistently and most adults at some time. Yuck!

What Causes Bad Breath?

Bad oral hygiene. The commonest cause of bad breath is neglecting your mouth, teeth, and gums. Everyone should brush their teeth immediately after a meal and use dental floss to remove food from between the teeth before it starts rotting. You wouldn't believe how many people don't clean their teeth regularly. Using a mouthwash or chewing sugar-free gum may help to freshen your breath.

Infections of the lungs and other medical conditions such as liver and kidney disease can be detected on the breath.

Bad Breath Tests

- **Lick your wrist.** Wait ten seconds, then smell it.
- **Ask your friends** for an honest assessment.
- **Ask your brother.** But be warned: he will reel back gasping, no matter how mountain-air fresh your breath is!

BALANCED DIET

See **Food and Nutrition: *What is a balanced diet?***

BIOLOGICAL CLOCK

You'll hear a lot of older women, and TV programs, talking about this. The biological clock is ticking for every woman. Girls are born with a set number of eggs in their ovaries and *never make any more. This means the older you get the older the eggs are getting and there are only a certain number of years in which you can conceive a baby.* Each month, from puberty to the menopause (between the ages of approximately 12–50), usually only one egg is released into the womb.

The best time for a woman to have a baby is when she is young, strong, and physically fit – probably from her early twenties to mid thirties. Because of the effects of hormones, a woman's breasts don't mature until she has had her first baby; and having one before the age of 30 helps to reduce the possibility of her getting breast cancer later. After 40, risks to the health of both mother and baby increase, especially the risk of the baby being born with Down's syndrome.

A young mother will have more energy than an older woman to bring up children (and the teenagers they will become) as well as maintaining her own interests and work. Before contraception became so efficient, women did tend to have children early but nowadays they can choose when to have a baby and sometimes they put it off too long and may find they have difficulties conceiving.

Some women think they'll get left behind in their career if they take time off work to have a baby, or perhaps they just don't find the right partner who wants to settle down and have a family with them. When you have a baby, it is natural for its welfare to become your top priority and you will *want* to enjoy the first years of its life. Somehow, because you have to, you will also find time and ways to care for it *and* do whatever else you want to do in life. And hopefully the baby's father will want to share in its upbringing and you can work out between you how to share the responsibilities of family life.

BLISTERS

Blisters are the bane of athletes' lives and for girls who insist on wearing some shoes that look fabulous but cause friction by rubbing against the skin. Blisters fill with a sterile fluid to protect the tissues of the foot. Contrary to popular belief, you shouldn't burst blisters because they can become infected and the healing process will be slower. It's best to leave them uncovered and wear shoes that won't aggravate them.

Tight 'n' Trendy

Squeeze your feet into trendy shoes that look great but are too tight and you're bound to get a painful blister or two. So, try to buy shoes that are not only trendy but fit well too.

Top Tip: Your feet swell during the day so buy your shoes in the afternoon.

BLOOD

See **Menstruation**.

BLOOD TYPES

There are three main blood types: A, B, and O. We each inherit a single blood type from our parents. Doctors must know your blood type if you need to have a transfusion because it is essential that you are given blood that matches your own. For example, if you needed blood after an accident, a small amount of yours would be taken from you and tested to see what type it is. Doctors don't expect you to remember what your blood type is because if you were given the wrong blood then you could die.

Each blood type can be RHESUS (RH) *positive* or *negative*. That is, it either contains a protein called rhesus or it doesn't. This is very important in pregnancy. If you are a rhesus *negative* mother and you have a baby who is rhesus *positive* then there's a risk that your body may produce antibodies to the blood of the baby inside you. This is not usually a problem with a first baby but with subsequent babies the mother has to be given an injection to protect the unborn child.

BLUSHING

I think we all know about this one. A bright red face is the last thing we want in an already embarrassing situation. I don't know the purpose of blushing and I don't think anyone else does either! But it's easy to explain. When you are anxious, a hormone called adrenaline is released from the adrenal glands above the kidneys. It causes the heart to beat faster, your breathing to increase, your body to perspire, and your face to blush bright red. This happens because the small blood vessels (capillaries) in the face dilate and blood rushes to the surface.

BODY ART

Decorating our bodies has a long tradition especially in some African tribes who have customs such as wearing many rings around the neck to stretch it, the patterns some Indian brides trace onto their hands with henna, and the body markings of the Australian Aborigines. Whatever inspired it, in the Western world it has now become very trendy to draw on your body. It can be either **permanent** or **temporary**.

Permanent Tattoos

Tattoos are *permanent*, which is why in Britain and the USA you have to be 18 to have one. They are made by injecting colored dye into the skin with a series of needles. And it does hurt! They used to be popular only for drunken sailors and bikers but recently tattoos have become a fashion fad. Many celebrities now boast a small tattoo on a hidden part of the body, such as the top of the shoulder or on the buttocks. But, remember, when they no longer want them *they* can afford the best medical treatment to have them removed.

I really regret my tattoos now. They must look really cheap.
I wish I'd listened to my mother.
Geri Halliwell (Ginger Spice)

Tattoos can look pretty when they are first done. The colors are bright and the designs can be wild. They can also have a special meaning, such as your boyfriend's name tattooed on your arm! And imagine having the name of your favorite pop star emblazoned across your chest. Great when you're young but how will it look when you're 65? The colors fade and quite soon they all merge into a horrible murky green. Inevitably, tattoos will go out of fashion and you could be left with a sheep on your cheek which is suddenly completely uncool.

Having a tattoo surgically removed is difficult, painful, expensive, and may permanently damage your skin.

Temporary Tattoos

The 1990's answer to body art, temporary henna tattoos get around many of the problems. They color the surface of the skin in the pattern of your choice. They have no after effects, so you can have all the fun of a tattoo without any trauma.

Body Piercing

Although you have to be 18 in Britain and the USA to have a

tattoo, there is no law about what age you can have body piercing. It's allowed with parental permission or if a child is considered responsible enough to make their own decision. Many parents loathe the idea of their child being pierced and wearing body rings. It may seem very cool to have rings in your eyebrows, nose, lips, tongue, belly button, and lots more besides, but the trend will soon pass and you could be left with little scars all over you.

Body piercing is a minor operation and must be carried out by a fully-trained person with sterile instruments to minimize the risk of contracting serious infections such as HIV and hepatitis. Ask if the person doing the piercing is insured to cover any medical costs that you might incur as a result of being pierced.

Body piercing can cause medical problems.

Infections caused by bacteria are common. A quarter of the people who have their tongue, navel, or ears pierced end up with them infected! The area becomes red, inflamed, and fills with puss. It usually requires removal of the offending body ring and a course of antibiotics.

Scarring is especially common in people of African origin due to a condition called keloid. The skin overgrows itself and forms unsightly lumps that are very difficult to remove.

Damage to body structure: Any of the underlying structures can be damaged. The bit that is pierced, such as the body's cartilage may become deformed. Arteries and nerves may be damaged which can lead to bleeding and a loss of sensation.

Make sure the right sized gun is used. If you pierce the belly button with an ear gun, for instance, the hole will be too narrow and the piercing will be too short. It won't allow for swelling and will have to be cut out because the skin will grow over it.

Yeouch!

I've seen a girl who was unlucky enough to rip out her belly-button ring by catching it on a door handle.

To reduce the possibility of allergic reactions and infections, wear jewelry made of surgical steel.

The tongue is a particularly dangerous area to have pierced. The risk of infection is high and if the tongue swells it can block off your air supply. I've also seen girls who have swallowed their tongue stud. In rare cases, if the piercing is not done properly, it can cause paralysis of the tongue.

BODY HAIR

As you grow from a girl into a woman, one of the most noticeable changes is the growth of body hair. It is quite normal for it to grow in your armpits, around your genitals (pubic hair), sometimes around the nipples, and on your legs and face. Some nationalities are naturally predisposed to have more facial and body hair than others. Every girl has different quantities and it only needs to be removed if you think it is excessive.

Pubic hair starts to grow approximately between the ages of 9-14 and stops growing when you're about 16. It's shorter, curlier, and thicker than the hair on your head because the hair follicles it grows from are a different shape.

Armpit and leg hair starts to grow later than pubic hair. In Western countries, most women choose to shave or use depilatory creams or wax to remove this hair as they think it is unattractive. Hair in the armpits traps the body's pheromones (natural smells

Dr. Dave's Top Tips – Unwanted Hair

Like most problems, there is always help available and getting this one sorted out immediately will save years of agony.

Creams and waxes can be used but they may cause irritation. Available from pharmacists, they can be self-applied or, if you have plenty of money, you can treat yourself to beauty parlor treatments.

Hairs can be bleached to make them less obvious. This should only be done by a trained professional or you could damage your skin. Beauty parlors and some hairdressers offer this service.

Hairs can be shaved. Always use a fresh disposable razor. Do it in the bath or shower and lather up first with your normal soap to raise the hairs. Shaving will *not* make the hairs grow back coarser.

Electrolysis is the application of a very weak electric current to each individual hair to destroy the follicle from which it grows. It will take a number of treatments but should permanently remove the hair. It should only be done by a specially trained beautician but is expensive because a number of sessions will be necessary. A cheaper option for self-treatment is a battery-driven applicator, available from pharmacists. Read and follow the instructions very carefully.

Your doctor will help if you think an imbalance of hormones is causing excessive hair.

that attract the opposite sex – yes, it's true!). When these natural body odors are broken down by bacteria they can smell unpleasant, but washing daily will keep you sweet!

Excessive facial hair in a women can be caused by an imbalance of hormones, especially if her body is producing too much of the male hormones. If you think you are growing more than a soft and normal down on your face, your doctor should be able to help you.

Excessive body hair can make you feel bad about yourself and you may want to hide your body, especially from the opposite sex. This won't be too much of a problem while you are young but when you are ready to start having physical relationships it could cause you real difficulties. Again, it is probably caused by an imbalance of hormones and your doctor should be able to help you.

Too Hairy?

If unwanted hair is getting you down, talk to your doctor or a trained beautician.

BODY IMAGE

Everyone wants a perfect body. Magazines are full of thin pretty models carefully photographed in perfect lighting to make them look gorgeous. This gives the rest of you girls an almost impossible ideal to live up to, unless of course you have masses of money and a team of people entirely devoted to your appearance!

Don't make yourself miserable longing to look like someone else. The beauty industry is out there making millions by convincing you their moisturizer, make-up, dye, exercise, etc., is going to magically turn you into a goddess. Take a look at yourself and try to like what you see. There will be lots of different images to experiment with that will make the most of your good points. Wear clothes and make-up that are fun and suit your life as a unique individual.

Whatever your ideal image, you are born with a genetic tendency to a particular shape. No matter how hard you try you'll only ever be able to modify it slightly. If you can be sure about yourself and what you look like, you'll be more confident, appear more attractive, and be happier. Try not to dwell on what you *think* is wrong with you. A smile on your face will distract most people from any tiny blemish that is bound to have grown completely out of proportion in your own mind.

BODY ODOR
See **Body hair: *Armpit, Deodorant.***

BOYS
As you grow older, your attitude to boys changes. Boys who were once friendly playmates, or even irritating and smelly little nuisances, suddenly become the most desirable creatures in the world without whom life wouldn't be worth living – or so many girls think!

Boys undergo both physical and mental changes during puberty. They grow rapidly in height; hair grows under their arms, on their chest, face, and groin. Their testicles enlarge and their penis grows to its adult size. Their muscles develop, they lose fat, and their voice cracks and deepens. They are just as uncertain about themselves as girls are, even those who put on a great show of bravado. They mature mentally as they progress through puberty although they do tend to be a year or two behind girls. Even at 17 or 18, they can still seem annoying and immature to girls of the same age.

Most teenagers are moody but unlike most girls who want to talk about what they feel, boys usually prefer to be left alone.

Being asked constantly what's wrong can irritate them. They either want to deal with it on their own or ignore it until it goes away. Boys tend to have less predictable mood swings than the regular monthly fluctuation of highs and lows that girls have due to their menstrual cycle.

Boys and girls are made for one another. This book has been telling you that the best thing about you is what you are naturally, and the same thing applies to boys. What is interesting about them is who they are as individuals, their maleness, and their male preoccupations which are likely to be different to yours. If you team up with a boy, it doubles the range of feelings, talents, and interests available to you both. What girls and boys are most intrigued by are the mysterious ways in which they are different to one another. Try to value those things in a boy. Don't expect them to be like your girlfriends. You will have plenty of girlfriends for that.

See also **Sex.**

BRACES FOR TEETH

Having to wear a brace is *not* the end of the world. Braces are used to straighten teeth that are growing crooked. It can take a number of years but when the brace is removed your teeth will look a whole lot better.

The good news is that braces are much less ugly and smaller than they used to be. Some dentists will even let you choose the color of the pads that go on the teeth. In fact, I've met two girls whose braces were the colors of their favorite football teams – there's no accounting for taste! Oh, and by the way, you can kiss with braces on.

BREAKFAST

You must eat breakfast. It is the most important meal of the day. I ignored this constant chant of my parents all through my teenage years. For me, missing breakfast meant an extra half hour in bed. It took me an hour to wake up and I struggled through school mornings in a daze, wishing I was back in bed. I had no energy at all until after the 11 o'clock break when I bought something sweet and sticky to eat. After the break I could concentrate but I never understood why.

Now I know. Most of us get about eight hours sleep a night; more if we're lucky. Your body has to survive and repair itself with no intake of food during that time. Your blood sugar drops and you need to refuel in the morning. Until you eat something, your poor body simply can't function at full capacity. There's a lot of sense in the old saying:

**Eat breakfast like an empress,
lunch like a princess,
and supper like a pauper.**

Recent research has found that children who eat breakfast do better at school and some schools even provide breakfast.

Give Yourself Time for Breakfast

To give your body a fresh start each day, drink a glass of water first thing when you wake. (See **Water**.) All families will have their own tradition of what to eat for breakfast but if you want something fast and nourishing on school days, nothing beats a bowl of cereal, milk, and maybe honey, and some wheat bread toast with the spread of your choice. Cereal makes a great breakfast and provides the vitamins you need and plenty of fiber. (See **Food and Nutrition: *Fiber, the body's broom*.**) Milk and yogurt are good sources of calcium to build your bones. A banana, apple, or other fruit on your cereal tastes great and is good for you too. Wholemeal or wheat bread toast also provides fiber and if you drink lots of fluid to help move it through the bowel you'll avoid getting constipated.

Try to allow 15 minutes to sit and eat breakfast but, if you are occasionally running late, at least grab a couple of pieces of fruit to eat on the way to school. If your household is really well organized and there are a number of co-operative teenagers, you could take it in turns to cook a delicious omelette, pancakes, toast, or even just prepare a simple cereal breakfast. That way, at least some of the days you will get a few extra precious minutes in bed.

BREASTS

Breasts are the first obvious sign that you are changing from a girl into a woman. Growth can begin any time between the ages of 9-15 and may continue until you are about 18. Breasts and nipples may itch or tingle as they develop but this stops when they're fully grown. One breast is often slightly bigger than the other. The size and shape of breasts, their nipples and surrounding areola varies from girl to girl. The shape and size of yours will be part of what is uniquely attractive about you, so never waste your time and energy wanting them to be like someone else's. Until your first pregnancy, your nipples will be pink. During pregnancy they tend to darken to the color they will remain for life.

Because teenage boys are both fascinated by and shy about girls' breasts they want to talk about them a lot of the time. This is not always possible, so they make jokes about breasts, give them ugly names, and tease girls. Like you, they are discovering all kinds of new feelings about the opposite sex and hopefully the banter is just a way of releasing some of the excitement and turmoil they feel. They will eventually grow up and you'll be able to have a good relationship with them again.

Of course, the essential function of breasts is to produce milk to feed a baby. The warmth and closeness of suckling at a breast gives a baby a real sense of security that will benefit it all its life. The first breast milk a baby sucks from its mother also provides vital antibodies from the mother which protect the baby.

Breast Health and Examination

The lives of many women have been saved because they have taken the precaution of regularly checking their breasts for any unusual lumps or other changes which might indicate cancer. When your breasts are fully grown it will be time to get into a routine of feeling and looking at them in front of a mirror so that you get to know how they normally feel. Women's breasts vary; some have lumpier breasts than others, so you need to get used to knowing what yours feel like. Older girls do sometimes develop lumps but they are *rarely* cancer. They are usually cysts (fluid-filled cavities) or mobile breast lumps which are known as breast mice. These are normal and easily dealt with but the take-home message is the same: if you find a lump, see a doctor who can tell you what it is. Every woman's breasts change throughout her menstrual cycle. They usually feel more lumpy and tender in the days leading up to menstruation and this is nothing to worry about. It is recommended as you get older that you regularly check your breasts for any unusual lumps, puckering of the skin, or changes in shape. Get a leaflet from your doctor, or women's health advisor. There are plenty of good books about women's health that will show you how to do a breast examination. Even when a lump is found it is usually quite harmless, but the earlier a cancerous lump is found, the sooner it can be prevented from spreading, and the greater your chances of living a long and healthy life.

See **Cancer**, and **Further Reading**.

Seriously Over-large Breasts

The breast tissue of some girls is hypersensitive to the hormone estrogen. This may cause their breasts to overgrow and become heavy and pendulous. They will need a good bra to support them. But a teenage girl who finds herself with enormous breasts may feel deeply embarrassed by them. Rather than letting them spoil her future, the girl should speak to her doctor or women's health advisor about the options available.

See **Cosmetic Surgery**, and **Further Reading.**

Bras

You don't really need a bra until your breasts have some weight in them. However, you may feel more comfortable undressing in public changing rooms if you are wearing one. When *you* feel you need one is the right time to buy your first bra. Find a bra that supports your breasts well. Sizes have a number and a letter, e.g. 32A. The number refers to your chest measurement and the letter to the size of the cup that holds the breast. A rough guide is to measure your chest size underneath your breasts, then again around the fullest part of your breasts. If there is a difference of about three-quarters of an inch (2 cm) you need an A cup; if the difference is one and half inches (4 cm) you need a B; and if the difference is about two and half inches (6 cm) you need a C cup. Many shops offer a measuring and fitting service.

BROKEN BONES

Accidents do happen. If you break a bone there will be a rush of shock and pain, followed by swelling, bruising and temporary loss of control over the broken limb (which can feel very weird). When you arrive at hospital, the damaged part will be X-rayed to give the doctor a picture of the break. Treatment will vary according to which bit you've broken and how badly. A leg would be set in plaster for approximately six weeks and you soon become an expert at walking with crutches. A finger may just be taped to the one next to it for a few weeks. Miraculously, new bone cells grow and knit the broken bones back together. You will probably have to do physiotherapy exercises every day which are important if you want to get back full use of your limb.

Too many X-rays over a lifetime can be dangerous, so you don't want to have more than are absolutely necessary. *Insist* the radiologist covers your ovaries to protect them from radiation at the time of the X-ray. Otherwise, it could spoil your chances of getting pregnant in the future. See **X-rays**.

BULIMIA
See **Eating Disorders**.

BULLYING
I've met children who were bullied so badly that they had to leave school and move to another district. It has even lead to some children committing suicide. Bullying is mean and cowardly and affects as many as one in twenty children, so if you are being bullied you are not alone.

It's often a doctor who first realizes someone is being bullied. Either the child pretends to be ill to get out of going to school or they have a real illness brought on by the bullying. The stress of being bullied can cause dramatic mood changes, loss of appetite, stomach pain, and can make conditions such as asthma and eczema worse.

Bullying can take many forms. It may be physical when bullies hit or kick you; or can be verbal when you are insulted and called nasty names. Another form of bullying is when some children are simply left out of everything or are completely ignored.

Who Gets Bullied? A lot of people are bullied at some time in their life. Often, it is because they seem different in some way to the other children. It can happen because you are good *or* bad at sport or you don't like it; or you get better grades than the bullies; or your clothes are not considered "cool" enough. Bullies

Even Dr. Dave was Bullied

It was horrible and I never really knew why the bullies chose to pick on me. I usually enjoyed school; I was hard working but I always had a laugh too. Perhaps the main reason was that at the time I hated playing sports. I told an adult what was happening and their support gave me the courage to ignore the bullying, which did eventually stop. If I hadn't told someone it may have been a completely different story. Later, I became a prefect and did my best to prevent bullying happening to other kids – and mostly succeeded!

In many ways having to cope with being bullied made me stronger. Because I had to stand up for myself I became more confident that I could look after myself. If it hadn't happened, I might have been a different person today. Perhaps I would never have had the confidence to go on TV, or write this book. Maybe I wouldn't have been so determined about getting into medical school. Who Knows?

may think you have an unusual body shape or color; or may tease you because you wear glasses, or have come to school in your rubber boots on a rainy day. It could be anything – or nothing. You might just be in the wrong place at the wrong time.

Why Do People Bully? It's often a sign of insecurity or anger. Bullies themselves have often been bullied or neglected – often at home – and it's their way of getting their own back. They need to take out their anger on someone and don't dare direct it at the person who deserves it – that is the person who has bullied them. Bullies often don't realize the depressing effect they have on their victim.

How to Combat Bullying: Some schools have introduced schemes to overcome bullying.

Bully boxes in which children can leave an anonymous note saying who is bullying whom so that teachers can take action to stop it and to protect the child being bullied.

Class discussions can be organized so that children and teachers can talk about bullying, the effect it has, and what they think ought to be done about it.

Older children can be appointed to look after younger children.

Closed-circuit television cameras have been installed in some school playgrounds.

If you are being bullied, see **Abuse: Verbal or emotional abuse; and Assertiveness**.

C

Can carrots help you see in the dark?

Carrots contain vitamin A which helps to make a chemical called rhodopsin. These are vital for the eyes to function well, especially in poor light. Other yellow, orange, and dark green vegetables such as spinach, broccoli, pumpkin and squashes also do wonders for your eyes.

CANCER

Cancer is very rare in young people but it does strike an unlucky few. Almost all of us know someone older who has or has had cancer. Because it causes many deaths it can seem very frightening. But cancer treatments are improving fast and more people are being cured of it or are living longer after treatment than they would have done a few years ago. Like any disease, it is easier to cope with if you understand it. Knowing what it is and what causes it may also help you to avoid it.

Cancer isn't a single disease. The term cancer describes what is happening when some of the body's cells begin to multiply out of control. Normally, body cells divide in a controlled way as new cells are needed to replace old ones. Sometimes this process can go wrong. The body seems to forget how to stop certain cells dividing and they go on multiplying out of control. This is cancer and once it forms in one organ, it may begin to invade other body tissue and surrounding structures. It can spread to the glands or lymph nodes; or spread through the blood stream to other organs, especially the liver and brain.

High Risk Factors

Cancer usually attacks later in life but if you take action now you can reduce your chances of getting it when you are older. Some cancers specific to women are breast cancer and cancer of the cervix. Some women are more at risk than others.

Breast Cancer: Women are more likely to get breast cancer later in life if:

> their mother or grandmother had it.
> they have not had a baby before the age of 30.
> they smoke.

Bowel Cancer is more likely to form in women who:

> don't eat enough fiber nor drink enough water.
> smoke.
> have certain other bowel conditions, such as polyps.
> have a family history of bowel cancer.

Cancer of the cervix is more likely to develop if a woman:

> has sex (without using condoms) when very young.
> has sex with many different partners (without using condoms).
> smokes.

Other generally accepted causes of cancer include:

➤ Not getting enough good fresh food to eat in childhood.

➤ Some viral infections.

➤ Exposure to chemicals in the environment, such as asbestos dust, metals, hydrocarbons, solvents and their vapors, tobacco smoke. So always take seriously health warnings about wearing masks and protective clothing wherever chemicals are in use. Ensure rooms are well ventilated when being painted or household cleaning products are used, and always hang your dry-cleaned clothes in the fresh air for some time before you wear them.

➤ Some natural toxins such as mould on foods, especially grains; burned or charred foods.

➤ Radiation: ultraviolet (over-exposure to sunlight, although a certain amount of sunlight is essential to your body and psychological well-being), gamma and X-rays.

➤ Immune system malfunction.

➤ Old age, but this failing of cell division is normal as we age.

➤ Free radicals which damage cells. These negative ions are produced by the sun, by smoking, and are in the environment. A healthy body can rid itself of most free radicals and limit their damage if lots of fresh fruit and vegetables are eaten, and we don't smoke.

Early Diagnosis Saves Lives

Early diagnosis of a cancer improves a person's chance of survival. If you are at all worried, go to a doctor immediately. See **Breasts: *Breast Health and Examination*.**

Treatment of cancer varies depending on which kind it is. There are three main options and often treatment includes them all:

surgery to cut it out before it spreads; chemotherapy (injections of toxic drugs to kill the cancer); and radiotherapy (use of X-rays to kill the cancer cells). The outcome of the treatment depends on the type of cancer, your age and general health. Certain types of lymphoma (cancer of the lymph glands) are completely curable and many cancers can be cured if they are caught early. It has been shown that patients who have a positive attitude recover better than those who don't.

CANDIDA ALBICANS

Candida albicans is a yeast whose presence in the body is normally kept in check by a healthy body. But if the immune system

Dr. Dave's Top Tips – Thrush

❥ See your doctor. Once diagnosed, it can be treated with an antifungal drug. This will relieve the symptoms and destroy most of the bacteria but you need to find the cause if you don't want it to come back again.

❥ If you haven't had a recent course of antibiotics, then look at the food you eat. Do you eat too many sweets, candies, sugary drinks, and desserts? Reduce the quantity, at least for as long as the irritation lasts, and preferably forever!

❥ Wear loose-fitting clothes rather than tights.

❥ Don't use perfumed bubble baths or deodorants on the affected area. A cupful of sea salt in your bath water may sooth the irritation.

❥ Wash regularly with unperfumed soap and water.

❥ See also **Food and Nutrition.**

is weakened (perhaps after an illness or a course of antibiotics) then the yeast may grow excessively and cause vaginal thrush. This intense itching of the vulva and soreness in the vagina may worsen at night and there may be a thick white vaginal discharge.

Yeasts, which thrive on sugars, like warm moist conditions to grow in. Inadequate diet, and poor hygiene also encourage their growth. Thrush is more common just before a period and often affects women who regularly wear tights or pantyhose which prevent air circulating freely around the affected area.

See **Thrush**.

CARBON MONOXIDE POISONING
See **Gas Fires**.

CELLULITE (FAT)
Cellulite is an unsightly rippled effect on fatty parts of the body, such as the thighs. It's completely normal for women to lay down fat below the surface of the skin. But if the body's connective tissues have become weakened the fat cells push up through it and cause a pitted effect. There are no quick fixes. Cellulite creams and other treatments will *never* get rid of it, no matter how expensive they are. They may *appear* to work by making the surrounding tissue swell up to look smooth – *temporarily*. The only way to reduce the amount of cellulite on your body is to eat a healthy balanced diet, and exercise regularly to increase the blood flow to the area and strengthen muscle tissue. If you eat healthily and not too greedily *most* of the time there will be no *excess* fat to be laid down.

See **Food and Nutrition: *What is a balanced diet?***

CERVIX
This is the neck-like opening into a woman's uterus (womb) situated at the top of the vagina. After sexual intercourse (without

a condom), male sperm enter the womb via the cervix in search of an egg to fertilize.

You may hear older women talking about "smear tests." Pre-cancerous cells can be detected on the cervix and it is recommended that all women once they start having sexual intercourse should have a smear test once a year or every six months if they change their sexual partner. These tests are quick, painless, and usually carried out by a trained nurse in your doctor's office or women's health clinic. Having many different sexual partners (without using condoms) is thought to increase a woman's risk of contracting cancer of the cervix.

CHILDREN AS CARERS

Many children find themselves having to care for a relative who can't take care of him- or herself. They cook, clean, do the washing, the shopping, and sometimes even wash and dress their own parent. While having all these adult responsibilities they also go to school and try to have some life of their own. It is a tremendous strain but they do manage, even though their school work does sometimes suffer. They tend to grow up a lot faster than their friends but it is only natural that they sometimes feel envious. Why should they have to be a carer and not their friends? Why should their friends be able to spend all their time playing and doing what they want after school, etc.?

Sometimes, no one knows a child is a carer. It may be difficult for them to talk about it because they fear their family might be broken up if anyone knew. Carers are sometimes bullied at school which is another reason they stay quiet about it. If the responsibilities are getting them down, there are people who will help out. Ask your teacher for advice about where to get help or call a child helpline.

If you have a friend who is a carer, try to think what it would be like to be in her shoes. Be sympathetic toward her, and help her when you see she needs you. One of the best things you can do is keep your friend in touch with what's going on in your world by telling her about it. See **Support Groups**.

CHOICES

Every day presents a multitude of choices to be made and each one has consequences. Make your choice. If it turns out to be the right one that's great; if it suddenly seems not such a great idea, then you can always choose again. Bit by bit you discover what's right for you. Choosing *not* to dwell on past mistakes and bad times and to take a positive attitude about new possibilities will always open whole worlds of exciting opportunities and be a lot more fun.

COLDS

See **Flu (Influenza) and colds**.

COLD SORES

Cold sores usually start with a tingling sensation in the skin at the corners of the lips. A cluster of tiny blisters appears, gets bigger, bursts, weeps, dries up, and disappears. They last about a week. Because the virus that causes them stays in your body for life, cold sores tend to recur whenever you are run down. This might be after an illness or a particularly tense or busy period when you haven't been getting enough sleep and haven't been eating properly.

Cold sores are caused by the herpes simplex-1 virus. You will almost certainly become infected with it if you kiss anyone who has an active cold sore. Squeeze their hand instead and wait till they're better!

Dr. Dave's Top Tips – Cold Sores

Don't share a towel with anyone who has an active cold sore, and certainly don't kiss them until it's completely better!

Try to keep healthy and avoid getting run down. Eat fresh fruit and vegetables every day. Foods rich in vitamin C, such as oranges, may help your immune system to fight them off.

Get plenty of sleep.

Don't touch the blisters.

Treat them early before they appear. As soon as you feel the tingling sensation, act immediately! Apply Acyclovir cream or other cream recommended by your doctor or pharmacist. Hopefully, this will prevent the cold sore from actually appearing. If you get cold sores, this is a good precaution to take before flying as traveling by plane often brings them out.

CONFLICT

Part of being young seems to be arguing with your parents, teachers, and friends. In fact, teenagers seem to relish a heated debate. Conflict is not only a result of the mood swings we all experience during puberty but also serves another useful purpose. Getting into conflict with other people sharpens our wits and helps us to establish who we are and what we think and believe. It helps us to realize what our views are on certain matters and helps us to understand more about ourselves as individuals. It also stimulates other people to express their point of view which may in turn add to and modify what we think. It's not possible or even wise to avoid all conflict, because as you experience such situations you will find ways of dealing with them that will help you in the future.

A sign of maturity is being able to appreciate another person's point of view (you don't have to agree with them) and then to disagree with them using logical and rational arguments. This takes practice. Try to find ways of defusing a situation. Find something in the other person's argument with which you can agree before putting your own thoughts across. This is better than just exploding with some ill-thought-out phrases or words and door slamming. If all else fails, just pause before you answer, count to ten and think what you are going to say, instead of jumping in feet first!

CONSTIPATION

Many girls suffer from constipation (difficult and irregular emptying of the bowel). Bowel habits vary enormously. Some people go to the toilet once every three days and others three times a day. Either of these and anything in between is normal. If you are waiting longer than three days, you are constipated.

Constipation can be extremely uncomfortable and if it's persistent it can create health problems such as irritable bowel syndrome. You feel bloated, you break wind (fart) a lot, and you can get terrible stomach pains. And if you sit on the toilet straining a lot, it can cause the bowel wall to weaken and bleed (a condition known as piles or hemorrhoids).

Causes of Constipation

Poor diet, lack of exercise, the side effects of some medicines, pregnancy, anxiety, stress, tension, and ignoring the desire to go to the toilet can all cause constipation. If you are staying away from home your stools may become hard or irregular but this will

Dr. Dave's Top Tips – Constipation

Eat more food that contains fiber, such as wholemeal or wheat bread and pasta, brown rice, beans, peas, lentils, cereal, fruit, and vegetables. See **Food and Nutrition.**

Eat more fruit. Prunes can help.

Drink lots of fluid, especially water. Try to avoid tea and coffee which are dehydrating.

Never ignore the urge to go to the toilet. When it comes – go! And try to get into a routine of going to the toilet at about the same time each day.

Find a way to relax if you're feeling pressured.

If you need help urgently, medicinal preparations are available from the pharmacist. Start with lactulose (which contains special sugars) and then use fybogel (fiber). If these don't work then you should see your doctor.

Glycerine suppositories can be inserted to soften hard stools but rather than become dependent on these, it is better to eat well and drink lots of water.

pass and you will be back to normal soon after you get into your own routine and eating habits again.

If you don't eat enough fiber, don't drink enough water, or ignore your bowel when it's telling you to go to the toilet, it becomes lazy. On its way from your mouth to your bottom food is squeezed through the whole length of the bowel by a muscular action of the bowel called peristalsis. For this process to work the food has to have bulk provided by fiber which is insoluble. It absorbs water, swells up and cleans up the bowel as it is pushed through carrying other waste matter with it.

When food enters the stomach it causes a reflex action. Approximately twenty minutes after you eat, the gastrocolic reflex occurs and the rectum (bottom end of the gut) is stimulated to contract and let you know you want to go to the toilet. If you don't go, the urge will pass. If you do this often enough, the reflex action will stop happening, the bowel will become lazy and stop functioning properly.

CONTRACEPTION

> *It couldn't happen to me.*
> # OH YES IT COULD!

**Every year, thousands of
girls under 16 get pregnant.**

I hope it's a long time before you have to worry about this but it is important that you know *now* about the issues involved. If people are going to have sex and don't want to get pregnant then they must use contraception (preferably with the male wearing a condom). The woman is the one who will carry a baby for nine months and be its mother for life if she gets pregnant. Theoretically, both the woman and the man should be jointly responsible for contraception. In reality, there is more at stake for a woman, who should make sure she is in control by having effective contraception.

Essential Guide to Contraception

It may seem unromantic but it is vital that a young woman gets all the information she can about contraception so that she can decide which method is right for her in her circumstances. She can get advice and leaflets from her doctor, a family planning clinic, or women's health advisor, and of course from library books and book stores. Some contraceptive methods are better than others.

Abstinence is 100 percent guaranteed.
If you don't have sex you won't get pregnant,
nor contract any sexually transmitted disease.

The Pill

Oral contraceptive pills are *almost* 100 percent effective at preventing pregnancy if taken as per instructions. It prevents women becoming pregnant by artificially altering their hormonal balance. It can also be taken to reduce period pain and premenstrual tension.

The pill does NOT protect a woman from getting HIV or other sexually transmitted diseases.

Condoms

Male condoms are almost 100 percent effective if used properly. Protection against pregnancy is increased if a condom is used *and* the woman is on the pill.

**ONLY CONDOMS
can protect against HIV and
other sexually transmitted diseases.**

A condom is a latex rubber covering which is put on the man's erect penis to prevent semen reaching the female genital tract during sexual intercourse.

Diaphragm (Cap)

If inserted properly and used with a spermicide gel the diaphragm is about 95 percent effective. *It does NOT protect a woman against sexually transmitted diseases*.

A diaphragm is a round latex rubber cap which fits snugly over a woman's cervix inside her vagina to prevent semen entering the womb.

Intrauterine Device (IUD) or Coil

These devices are very effective at preventing pregnancy but *offer no protection from sexually transmitted diseases*. They come in many different shapes. One is placed inside the uterus (womb) by a qualified medical practitioner and if it causes no trouble can stay there for years. Because the body recognizes there is something foreign in the womb it prevents the implantation of an egg.

Natural or Rhythm Methods

A woman can get pregnant only during a certain few days in the middle of her menstrual cycle (between periods). This is when an egg has been released from one of her ovaries to travel along the Fallopian tube into the womb. Theoretically, if a woman avoids having sex during the days when an egg is available to be fertilized she shouldn't get pregnant. However, many people are alive today who wouldn't exist if this method were reliable!

Emergency Contraception

If a woman has had unprotected sex, emergency contraception is available to abort a possible pregnancy. The pills must be taken within 72 hours of having sex; so she should see a doctor the next day. Two pills containing a high dose of estrogen are taken, followed by two more twelve hours later. They may cause nausea and vomiting. Day-after pills are a last resort and should not be used as routine contraception. *They do not provide protection against HIV or other sexually transmitted diseases.*

COSMETIC SURGERY

This is not something that should be undertaken lightly. It is often painful, hugely expensive, can go badly wrong, and doesn't always achieve the desired result. Plenty of private clinics make a fortune out of women's sense of insecurity about their looks. Some celebrities have famously had cosmetic surgery. They have enormous amounts of money to pay for the very best treatment yet even they often end up looking sadly disfigured.

A teenage girl should not even think about having cosmetic surgery just for the sake of some fad or fashion; such as injections to increase her lip size or altering her breasts. None of us are physically perfect and our minor imperfections are often what is uniquely attractive about us. However, if for example you have ears that do really stick out and it's really getting you down then perhaps you should speak to your doctor and ask to be referred to a surgeon who is an expert in that particular operation. See also **Breasts: *Seriously Over-large Breasts***; and at the end of this book under: **Support Groups: Cosmetic Surgery – *Find an Expert***.

CRAMPS

When a muscle goes into spasm it is called cramp. Cramp can be agony, especially in the middle of the night if it grips the calf muscles of your leg and your toes. During any fast or prolonged exercise the body loses moisture and salt and this dehydration can cause cramp; also lactic acid builds up in the muscles and needs time to disperse. Cramps are more likely if you don't warm up gently before vigorous exercise and wind down slowly after it. Some girls suffer from cramp of the lower abdomen during menstruation. Because the body needs its energy to digest food, swimming less than an hour after a meal can result in stomach cramp.

See **Water: *Dehydration***.

Dr. Dave's Top Tips – Cramp

Drink 6-8 glasses of water during every day and a glassful before bed.

Leg Cramp

➤ You'll probably wake everyone in the house with your screams of pain, so get one of them to gently massage the offending muscle. Then slowly and gently push the toe end of your foot up and down until the muscles relax. The foot needs to be held in each position for a minute or two. Gradually the muscles will relax.

➤ Run some hot water into the bath and stand in it with your foot curving up the side of the bath.

➤ Drink some water with a pinch of salt in it.

➤ Take a hot water bottle back to bed with you to keep the muscle warm.

➤ Avoid sitting with your legs in awkward positions.

➤ Do some leg-stretching exercises before bed.

Exercise-related Cramp

➤ Drink a glass of water before doing any intense exercise.

➤ Warm up with gentle stretching exercises before a period of intense exercise and gently wind down afterwards rather than suddenly just stopping.

➤ After vigorous exercise, have an isotonic drink such as diluted fruit juice or special sports drink to replace the moisture and salt your body has used up.

CRUSHES

Teenagers often develop a crush on someone of the same sex. It might be a teacher, or a girl at school. You admire the person tremendously, think about her all the time, long to be like her, want to be near her and for her to like you. These feelings of love and admiration are very real and strong and can last for months or years, but then you begin to notice *boys* and how attractive they have suddenly become!

CYSTITIS

Most women have a bout of cystitis once in their lives, others get this infection of the bladder repeatedly. It is caused by a bacterium that normally lives in the bowel. If it gets into the urethra (the tube that carries urine out of the body) it can cause an infection which

---

Dr. Dave's Top Tips – Cystitis

Avoid getting dehydrated. Drink at least 8-10 glasses of water every day. This will help flush out the bacteria.

Avoid fresh fruit juices which are very acidic.

Bath or shower every day but don't have long hot bubble baths, nor use perfumed bath gels or use vaginal deodorants.

After going to the toilet, wipe yourself from front to back.

Wear cotton pants and loose natural fiber clothing because wearing tight trousers, synthetic pants and tights creates a warm moist atmosphere in which bacteria can thrive.

If you have sex, urinate and wash immediately afterwards.

---

makes it sting horribly when you pee. This pain is caused by more-than-usually acidic urine as it passes through the inflamed urethra. If it is not treated the infection can move up through the bladder and into the kidneys. So see a doctor. If you have cystitis, go to the library or a book store and find out as much as you can about it so that you can take steps to avoid it in the future.

Are We Born Deaf or Made Deaf?

Some children are born deaf, but hearing can be badly damaged by constant loud noise, such as listening to music too loud on a personal stereo.

DANCING

I love dancing. Not only is it great fun but it's great for burning off loads of calories, keeping you fit, and letting off emotional steam! The exercise also releases natural chemicals in your brain that make you feel good. The only downside is that you will often be dancing in a smoky atmosphere and gasping in more smoke than a smoker. Dance till you drop but always drink plenty of water so you don't get dehydrated.

Ballet dancers have some specific problems. They need to be fantastically fit and must eat properly to provide their body with the energy it burns up. There's massive pressure on them to be very thin – many of the dancers I know are bordering on becoming anorexic. Also, because they work their body so hard they tend to get a lot of painful joint problems.

DANDRUFF

It's normal to have old skin cells flaking off your scalp; it's only a problem if there's a great deal of it. Recent research has shown that people with dandruff have a visitor on their scalp – a yeast called *Pityrosporum ovale*. There are many anti-dandruff shampoos on the market and some will work better for you than others. Try some that contain selenium. If they don't help, then ask the pharmacist for one that contains *Zinc pyrithione* which kills yeasts. If this doesn't work then your doctor can prescribe something stronger. And don't forget to drink plenty of water, in case dehydration is part of your dry scalp problem.

DATING

Girls often ask how old they should be before going on a date. I don't think there can be any rule about this as every circumstance is so different. It's probably OK if you have known the boy as part of a group of friends for years before you go out alone with him. If he's a complete stranger then arrange to meet first in some public place where you will be safe and can get to know him and *importantly* he gets to know you as a valuable individual. If you like and trust the boy, and feel you want to go out with him, then go, but make sure you know what *you* want the limitations to be. One way of making sure you aren't caught out is to think about the issue before you go, otherwise you may do something in the heat of the moment that you regret later. And always carry enough money to get home alone if you have to.

DECISIONS

I think decisions are exciting, but scary too. Every time you have a big decision to make it's like standing at a crossroads; the direction you take alters your life forever!

If you decide to get a job rather than go to college your life will be utterly different to what it might have been. You'll meet a set of people who will link you to all kinds of different interests and directions; but you may have fewer choices about making a career. Or if you decide to hang out rather than play tennis you might miss out on meeting someone really special at the tennis court. On the other hand, someone who could become a really good friend or change the direction of your life might bump into you on the bus to the shops. Weird!

To make a big decision, gather all the information you need about the various options and consider it. If it's a really big decision, perhaps discuss it with someone who has had more experience. Think about the pros and cons of each option (write them down if you need to); perhaps have a night's sleep so your subconscious mind can work on it too, then *decide*.

Spontaneous decisions can often be best! Clothes shopping is a classic example. You see something, you want it, you just know it's right, you buy it and it's a great decision. Other times you just can't decide whether to have one top or the other and you waste hours getting totally frustrated. You finally decide on one, but go home still worrying that perhaps you've made a mistake!

The important thing is to make a decision. If it doesn't work out, it's a waste of time and energy getting depressed or upset about it. At least it's eliminated one option and you can move on to your next set of options far more quickly than if you were still dithering around trying to make the first decision.

DEHYDRATION

See **Water,** one of the most important entries in this book.

DEODORANT

There is nothing worse than sitting on a bus next to someone with terrible body odor. After puberty, glands in your armpits secrete sweat, especially when you're hot or embarrassed. Sweat itself doesn't smell but bacteria love it and merrily convert it into other chemicals that do smell. If you want to smell sweet all day long, wash regularly and use a roll-on deodorant. Spray-on deodorants work just as well but you do inevitably inhale some of the spray. Deodorants are essentially smelly chemicals that mask the smell of sweat. Antiperspirants work by reducing the amount of sweat that can be secreted. However, it is natural for the body to sweat so perhaps antiperspirants aren't such a great idea; but there's no evidence that they are bad for you.

We smell for a very good reason. Our natural smell is one of the many things that makes us attractive to one another. The smell of someone you really like can literally make you go weak at the knees!

DIETING

> CHILDREN AND TEENAGERS SHOULD *NEVER* DIET.

If you are overweight, you probably eat too much of the wrong kind of food. Discover how eating plenty of delicious foods will keep you in shape and be far less bother than any diet, see **Eating Disorders;** and **Food and Nutrition,** especially *What is a balanced diet; Foods you'd be better off without.*

DISCO DEAFNESS

Most of us love our music LOUD. But it can seriously damage your hearing. Personal stereos can deliver *over 100 decibels* of sound directly into your ears, and music at discos and pop concerts can be even louder. This is how it compares to other noise levels:

- **80 decibels:** A busy room with lots of background noise.
- **105 decibels:** Some types of road hammer drill. By law, anyone who uses one has to wear ear protection.
- **150 decibels (Ouch!):** A jet aircraft.

Sound travels through the outer ear to the ear drum which vibrates. This moves three bones (hammer, anvil, and stirrup) in the middle and transmits the sound to the spiral inner ear which is covered in tiny hairs. These sensitive hairs convert the sound into nerve impulses that travel to the brain.

Very loud sound damages these hairs causing ringing in the ears and muffled hearing. After a night at a loud disco or concert, one in five teenagers complain of ringing in their ears the next day – their hearing is temporarily damaged. If you constantly bombard your inner ear with loud noise this ringing sound (tinnitus) can become permanent. Imagine if every single second, day and night, for the rest of your life you had to put up with a ringing sound in your head!

Everyone's hearing begins to fail as they age but the more you damage it when you're young, the earlier you'll lose your ability to hear well.

Dr. Dave's Top Tips – Hearing

The best advice is to enjoy the music but protect your hearing.

At concerts or discos take a ten minute break from the music every hour, or wear earplugs.

Turn your personal stereo down. It's too loud if the person next to you can hear it.

DIVORCE OR SPLITTING UP

Divorce or splitting up is dreadful for the adults involved but their children also suffer because they feel torn between being loyal to them both. They usually love both parents and hate the thought of them not all living together.

**It's not your fault if your parents
no longer want to live together.**

For whatever reason parents decide to split up, if they have totally lost sympathy for one another it may be better than struggling on for years in a house full of ghastly arguments and horrible tension. They'll be terribly worried about what is best for their children, so splitting up is not a decision they make lightly. Once they decide, it's unlikely you could ever make them change their minds.

I think the best thing to do is to try not to get involved in the arguments. Tell them you'd rather they stayed together but you will accept whatever decision they make. Try not to take sides or play them off against each other saying things like, "Dad said I could stay out till 10," even if he didn't. Every situation is different. You may get dragged into arguments or unfairly shouted at as they release some of their anger and frustration. On the other hand, you may not get any attention at all because they're too busy screaming at each other.

If you like both your parents, hopefully they will choose new partners who you can also like. Try not to stubbornly insist on hating them. They didn't break up your home, your parents chose to do that to make their life and yours better.

It can be very worrying if you don't have anyone outside the situation to talk to about your fears and what is happening at home. Talk to your brothers and sisters if you have them. Don't be shy about talking to a friend about it or perhaps a friend's mother if she's a good listener. Or look in the local phone directory for a child helpline to call. You will find someone kind and helpful on the line and what you talk about will be completely confidential. See **Support Groups.**

Most kids I've spoken to say what got them through it all was concentrating on the positive aspects. After the divorce there is less tension in the house even though you might be poorer. You have more time with each parent paying attention to you. You have two places to live. You have twice as many people who care about you and you get more presents. You may even get more freedom and more visits to interesting places and . . . two sets of holidays!

Parents splitting up may be painful and turbulent for a while but things do settle down and work out in the long run.

DOCTORS

Some girls prefer to have a female rather than a male doctor, especially for "female" problems. Male doctors will know just as much about female conditions but if you would feel happier with a woman doctor you should be able to find one. As you grow up you may decide to change from your family's doctor. Most group practices have more than one doctor so you can always ask to see a different one or try other practices. Find a doctor who you like and trust, and feel able to talk with openly.

Doctors are extremely busy and sometimes patients feel they've been rushed out of his office before they've told the doctor everything they wanted to. So, prepare yourself beforehand by writing down your symptoms and any questions you want to ask. Refer to your notes when you visit the doctor. If you don't understand what your doctor says, then say so! And ask if they could explain it more simply. If drugs are prescribed ask if there are any side effects you should know about.

If you have a medical problem, see your family doctor first. If a general practitioner thinks you need to be seen by a specialist he or she will refer you to one. If you have an accident or other emergency you will probably be taken direct to the accident and emergency or casualty department of a hospital.

If you have found what you've read in this book really interesting you may like the idea of becoming a doctor or nurse or some other kind of care worker. Such careers are very demanding but also enormously satisfying. Ask at school how you can find out what subjects you will need to take to get into medical school because *now* is the time to start directing your education. It will also help to give a sense of purpose to what you are studying.

See also **Find Out for Yourself.**

DREAMS

Everyone dreams when they sleep. Even though they can be fantastically vivid and complex at the time we often can't remember them when we wake up. It isn't yet fully understood what is happening in our brain when we dream. It's thought that our subconscious mind is processing everything we've experienced while awake, making sense of it, storing important bits in our memory and getting rid of rubbish. Dreams often seem to spring from something you've noticed during the day. They're often confused and don't always make logical sense. Some people say dreams predict the future but there's no evidence to prove it. Some of us have recurring dreams or nightmares in which we experience the same events night after night, such as falling, flying, or being chased.

Daydreams are different. You have them while you're awake, so they're not really dreams. They happen when you stop concentrating and your imagination takes over. They often happen when you're bored, like in assembly at school.

See also **Sleep.**

DRESSING UP

It's great to look the part when you go out. If you look really good you'll feel good and confident. There's nothing like experimenting and being inventive with the way you look – and looking great. Some girls love to spend hours (days even!) preparing their outfit, their hair, and their make-up for a night out. When you put so much effort into something, you want to be noticed.

What you wear sends out great flashing messages about who you are, so young girls need to be a bit careful about the kind of signals their clothes are giving out. The latest cool trend may be bare bellies, skin-tight tops, and short skirts which are wonderful but not always appropriate to where you will be. You may not always welcome the kind of attention you get. So, as well as thinking about what you wear, think about the messages it will be sending out.

DRUGS

They're everywhere. Drugs are being pushed in most towns and cities, often to quite young children. If *you* haven't already been offered some you almost certainly will be one day. If you are tempted to experiment you will be taking a massive risk.

**Drugs can destroy your life the very first time
you take a pill or sniff a powder. Or they
may just slowly wreck it.**

Over 100 teenagers have died recently as a result of taking ecstasy tablets. You could be next!

I've compiled a list of the most common drugs in circulation and what you need to know about them. Any one or all of these could be offered to you today or tomorrow. Make sure you understand the risks. I've included some current street names (but new ones are invented all the time), what they look like and what they do to you.

DON'T BE AN INNOCENT VICTIM.
Know what drugs can do to you before you're tempted.

AMPHETAMINES

Street Names: Uppers, speed, sulphate, whiz, purple hearts.
Form: Usually a white or grey powder or pills.
How used: Snorted (sniffed), swallowed, injected, or smoked.
Effects: These stimulant drugs take 4-6 hours to work. Effects last 3-4 hours. *It takes two days to recover from amphetamines.* They cause the user to become confident and alert with an excessive energy boost; eliminate feelings of tiredness and hunger.
Side Effects: Tiredness; depression; irritability; long-term insomnia (inability to sleep); loss of appetite; intense anxiety; hallucinations and paranoia (e.g., intense fear and certainty that you're being followed by people who want to hurt you); psychological addiction.

AMYL NITRATE

Street Names: Poppers, rush, locker room.
Form: Clear liquid.
How used: Inhaled.
Effects: A rush, feeling of light-headedness.
Side Effects: Headache, vomiting, skin rash, blood disorders.

BARBITURATES

Street Names: Barbs.
Form: Pills, capsules, solutions, syrup.
How used: Swallowed, injected, inserted in rectum.
Effects: Cause user to feel high, contentment, free of inhibitions.
Side Effects: Cause the breathing rate to drop and can lead to lung failure. User can become very emotional, disoriented, or aggressive. Overdoses are common, especially if taken with other drugs or excessive alcohol which can lead to coma and death. Dependence: habit-forming. User becomes tolerant of drug and needs to have them or they feel ill, anxious, irritable, and shaky.

BENZODIAZEPINES (tranquilizers)

Street Names: Tranx, jellies, eggs, downers.
Form: Pills.
How used: Swallowed or injected.
Effects: Relieve anxiety, make user feel calm and on a *high.*
Side Effects: User becomes tolerant to the drug and needs to take increasing amounts to have the tranquilizing effect. Dependency: habit forming. User needs the drug or they feel very ill, have difficulty sleeping, feel anxious, have tremors, and become very irritable.

CANNABIS

Street Names: Marijuana, pot, blow, hash, weed, ganja, dope, grass.
Forms: Cannabis may be a lump of brown resin, a plant (known as grass), or an oil.
How used: Smoked with tobacco or eaten.
Effects: User feels relaxed and giggly, perhaps with mild hallucinations. Effects vary. Some users get aggressive or extremely anxious.
Side Effects: Clumsiness; short term memory loss; psychological addiction. Slow reactions and poor concentration for some hours after taken (so it's best not to drive with anyone who has been smoking dope. Long-term side effects are uncertain. Cannabis may cause lung disease and possibly lung cancer.

COCAINE

Street Names: Coke, snow, charlie, freebase, rock, wash, crack.
Form: White powder or nuggets.
How used: Snorted; injected; or white nuggets (crack) are burned and inhaled.
Effects: This powerful stimulant produces self-confidence, exhilaration, and a feeling that there's nothing you can't do, Effects last up to an hour.
Side Effects: Hallucinations, paranoia, agitation and feeling sick. Increased pulse rate and blood pressure put strain on the heart. Snorting cocaine damages membranes of the nose making it dribble permanently. Moderate physical addiction: withdrawal symptoms may include severe tiredness, apathy, depression. As users become tolerant

to cocaine they need increasing amounts to get *high*, and it's enormously expensive.

Crack is a more addictive form of cocaine. It gives a faster and greater high but it doesn't last as long.

ECSTASY

This is still *the* drug of the moment, although users are starting to mix ecstasy with other drugs which is ***really dangerous.***

Street names: Ecstasy is named according to its color. A red and black capsule is called a *Dennis the Menace*; a yellow and green one is called a *rhubarb and custard*. There are hundreds of other names, including *New Yorkers* and *Love Burgers.*

Form: Capsules or tablets of different sizes which can be any color.

How used: Swallowed.

Effects: A *rush* of feeling which lasts 5-8 hours. The user feels as if they love everyone. Senses are intensified: sounds seem louder, colors brighter. It gives the user lots of energy which is why it is used as a dance drug. But actually these feelings are not real – they are simply manic and dangerous.

Side Effects: Ecstasy raises heart rate and blood pressure so much it can stop the heart. It has been known to kill people this way. It causes body temperature to rise often to dangerous levels. It also causes kidney, liver and brain damage. Long-term effects are not known although some experts think it may lead to a loss of memory and possibly dementia.

ECSTASY CAN BE FATAL IF TAKEN WITH ALCOHOL. ECSTASY USERS MUST DRINK A PINT OF WATER AN HOUR AND *NO MORE*. IF THEY DRINK TOO MUCH WATER THAT CAN ALSO KILL THEM.

HEROIN

Street Names: smack, scag, H, gear, brown.

Form: White powder. Sold in small folded pieces of paper called wraps.

How used: Smoked, inhaled, injected.

Effects: User feels very safe, as if wrapped in cotton wool.

Side Effects: Highly addictive. Users suffer terrible withdrawal symptoms (high temperature, sweating, vomiting, and diarrhea) if they don't use the drug regularly. Injecting heroine puts user at risk of contracting hepatitis, HIV infection, gangrene, and abscesses.

LSD (lysergic acid diethylamide)

Street Names: Acid, tabs, trips, blotters, dots.
Form: Tiny squares of blotting paper that have been impregnated with LSD. They often have cartoon characters printed on them.
How used: Swallowed.
Effects: Hallucinations (like dreaming whilst awake). Some of the dreams are good but others become awful nightmares known as *bad trips.*
Side Effects: Paranoia; psychological addiction. Users become tolerant of the drug and need increasing amounts for it to work. Flashbacks of the nightmares can recur anywhere, any time after taking LSD and can be *very* scary.

MAGIC MUSHROOMS

Street Names: Not known.
Forms: Mushrooms.
How used: Eaten raw or cooked, or made into tea.
Effects: Hallucinations with happy dream-like feeling.
Side Effects: Eyesight problems. Stomach pains, nausea, and vomiting. Risk of poisoning if user eats the wrong species of mushroom.

SOLVENTS

Solvents tend to be used by some younger children who often don't realize how dangerous they are.
Form: Lighter fuels, aerosols, glues, thinners, and correcting fluids can all contain solvents.
How used: Inhaled.
Effects: User feels high or woozy as if very drunk.
Side Effects: Breathing rate slows. User becomes drowsy, vomits, and can lose consciousness. Many users accidentally die of suffocation. Solvents can cause heart, kidney or liver failure.

Everyone reacts differently to drugs but they all have side effects. Using any drug is extremely risky as you can have no idea how it will affect *you*. Any drug can cause you to have a terrifyingly bad trip, even the first time you use it.

**Mixing drugs is even more dangerous
and can have devastating consequences.**

Drug pushers will often *give* you the first drugs *free* to get you hooked. Once you're addicted to a drug you are at the pushers' mercy because you will do and pay almost *anything* to get more of it. You may be risking your life by taking a drug but if you become addicted you could soon find yourself turning to crime to get money. This is how many girls have been forced into prostitution.

**NEVER BELIEVE A DRUG PUSHER!
They want you hooked so they can
make money out of you. They won't
care if you die in the process.**

I *really* hope you will think very seriously about the possible consequences and decide *not* to take drugs. Think about it now so you know what to say if you're ever offered any.

If you're worried about drugs and need help, there are free confidential drug counselors you can phone. Check your local phone book for support groups.

See also **Addiction, Smoking, Willpower**, and **Support Groups**.

Early Death

I once saw a 15-year-old anorexic girl collapse outside a cinema. As a result of losing so much weight her blood chemistry had changed and she'd had a heart attack. Despite my efforts and those of the ambulance crew, she died. What a tragic waste.

EATING DISORDERS

Anorexia Nervosa

Girls with anorexia nervosa obsessively starve themselves, almost to the point of death, usually because they *wrongly* believe they are fat. This is known as having an *altered body image*. Some girls also do excessive amounts of exercise and burn off yet more calories. As they lose weight they become increasingly tired and ill, and if their weight falls below 7 stone (98 lbs), they stop having periods.

Anorexia is serious and girls rarely get themselves through it without help. If you or any of your friends have a problem about eating, it is vital for you to get professional help as soon as possible. An anorexic needs to talk about and understand why she is not happy with who she is and the way she looks. Speak to an adult you trust, such as a parent, teacher, or doctor, or call a confidential helpline for advice. It's not grassing on your mate; she may need help but can't see it.

See **Food and Nutrition**, and **Support Groups** at the end of this book.

**Two percent of anorexics
die every year.**

Bulimia

Bulimics tend to binge on food and then make themselves vomit afterwards by sticking their fingers down their throat. They eat as much as they can cram in, almost until they feel ill, then feel very guilty and make themselves vomit. Binge eating is very dangerous as it can cause rupture of the stomach and again it can change the body's blood chemistry. Like girls who are anorexic, bulimic girls need to get help to sort out their psychological problems.

See also **Anorexia**, and **Support Groups.**

EDUCATION

If you are going to have the best choices in life, get as good an education as you can. You may think what you're learning at school is irrelevant to your life, but everything you learn and how you develop your skills to research anything you do want to know about will certainly be of benefit to you some time in the future. If for some reason you can't finish your education, don't give up hope of ever doing it. You can always study as a mature student later.

ENDOMETRIOSIS

The commonest symptom is abnormal pain before a period. It can block the Fallopian tubes which causes infertility and affect the functioning of the ovaries. It can cause heavy periods and/or constant pain in the lower abdomen.

So what is it? The uterus (womb) is made up of special tissue which changes in response to the female hormones and the monthly cycle (see menstruation). This tissue should stay within the walls of the uterus but sometimes doesn't. This is endometriosis in which pieces of uterine tissue are found in other places such as the ovaries, between the uterus and the rectum and in the pelvis. It is not known why this happens but it may be that the normal monthly period flows the wrong way. Instead of out through the cervix into the vagina during menstruation, the blood tissue may flow along the Fallopian tubes and out into the pelvic area.

Because it is special tissue it still reacts to the female hormones just as it did when it was part of the uterus. It swells up, then later it starts to bleed and causes blood filled pouches or cysts. The body doesn't like this and scar tissue starts to form between these areas causing the above symptoms.

It is diagnosed from the patient's description, along with an examination of the vagina. A special investigation called a laparoscopy can confirm diagnosis. This is done in a hospital or clinic by a gynecologist (specialist in female reproductive system) who inserts a tiny telescope through the wall of the abdomen to look at the uterus and ovaries.

It should be treated by a gynecologist who will have the option of prescribing various types of pills and medication or referring the patient for surgery to remove the tissue.

EXAM STRESS

The word *exam* strikes fear into the hearts of most school pupils. I detested exams at school and they continued to terrify me all through medical school. I've done more than my fair share so know quite a bit about them! Exams are horrible but you have to do them to get the job or university place you want. The sad thing is some people are good at exams and others aren't. But don't despair, exam stress is something you can learn to control.

It's good to be concerned about exams because it forces you to do some work. But if you worry too much you won't be able to study even when you want to. Girls have added problems because some of them suffer badly from pre-menstrual tension or from excruciating pain while menstruating (5+ days each month) and it's hard to concentrate if you're feeling low.

What you feel during exam time is completely normal. When you are anxious or scared, adrenaline is released from small glands above your kidneys. A small amount of this adrenaline improves your performance and concentration but too much of it can make you over anxious and things can go horribly wrong: the heart beats faster, you may sweat, blush, or shake, and your breathing may speed up. You could feel sick, vomit, or have diarrhea. Many people also find sleeping is difficult at this time.

**The best way to cope with
exam stress is to plan ahead.**

Dr. Dave's Top Tips – Exams

Quality of studying is always better than quantity, so:

Plan your studying: Give yourself plenty of time before an exam and set realistic targets for what to study each day (and do it). You'll take in and remember more if you study over a long period. You won't remember much if you try to cram it all in at the last minute because there will be too much pressure on you and that makes stress worse.

Study in a private space where you will not be distracted by anyone or anything. Turn off the television, radio, and the music you'd rather be listening to!

Eat and drink sensibly: Your body and your brain need energy to work and that comes from food. A well-balanced diet is essential to keep your body and mind healthy and in top shape. You can boost your energy with sugary snacks like chocolate during the exams. Coffee also gives some people an energy boost and may make you more alert, but it also adds to your body's stress levels. Drink a glass of plain water before going into an exam so that you are not dehydrated. See also **Water**.

Exercise may seem to be the last thing you want to do when studying time is running out, but it does help. Take a brief exercise break in the fresh air at least once every couple of hours or you may find yourself dozing off over your books. The exercise will refresh you and you'll be able to take in far more when you return to your desk. See also **Exercise**.

Sleep is vital. During bouts of studying and exams try to go to bed at a time that allows you to get as much sleep as you need to feel alert each morning. Also you need time to eat a good breakfast and not to have to leave in a rush to get to school on time. Arriving in a panic is not the best way to start an exam day. If you're studying, don't stay up too late; nor go to bed too early or you will just lie in bed getting anxious instead of sleeping.

If you're really worried, it can be a relief to talk to friends or parents about it. But try not to add their fears or anxieties to your own! Do your best to keep your mind calm so you can focus clearly on the task ahead.

You can only do your best. If you've worked hard and understood what you've been studying over the previous term or year, you should perform well in exams. Of course, it will also depend on the questions you're asked and perhaps even the state of your health and hormones on the day. In my experience, the people who fail exams are usually those who haven't done enough work.

Plan well and GO FOR IT!

EXERCISE

Modern children are doing less exercise than ever and girls are doing even less than boys. Some girls do less than a brisk ten-minute walk a day. And who can blame them? There's cars and buses to travel in, loads of great TV to watch, outfits to plan, friends to hang out with, movies to see; and many of you would rather do anything else other than play organized school sports.

So What? Well, if you don't exercise, you start to build up problems for later in life. Fat starts to be laid down in your arteries, making it more likely you'll get heart disease when you're older. You may become overweight and that causes many health problems. Exercise stimulates the body to function efficiently. It improves our mood and concentration and makes bones strong and healthy.

But I hate sports. The great news is you don't have to go to the gym or do twenty press-ups every day. Just do what you enjoy! There must be something here you like doing:

DISCO DANCING   SWIMMING   BADMINTON

ROLLERBLADING   SQUASH   RUNNING

CYCLING   TENNIS   5-BALL JUGGLING

Most importantly, if you enjoy your exercise you are more likely to do it again. You only need to get out of breath for about ten minutes a day to really notice the benefits.

And you won't waste a minute of precious time if you incorporate exercise into your normal routine. Walk or run up stairs rather than take the elevator. Cycle or walk fast to school rather than go by car.

EYES

We all look at one another but only *really* make contact if we look at or into one another's eyes. I was once told that eyes are the only part of the brain you can see, and it is sort of true. Eyes are a great indicator of what kind of person someone is and what mood or emotional state they are in. From the way a person looks at you, it is usually possible to know if they are energetic, bored, excited, happy, sad, tired, sincere or telling lies, have a sense of humor, and much else. From the amount of eye contact you have with them you'll know if they are shy or confident. You can often tell if they are trustworthy or a person to avoid.

Humans have the most amazing binocular vision. We don't see objects as if they were flat (like a photograph), we see in three dimensions (3D), and we need two eyes to do it. If you lose the sight in one eye you lose this ability and will not be able to judge distances.

Eyes are fragile and need to be looked after. If you work with machinery (perhaps at school or even cutting the grass!); ride on the back of a motorcycle, etc, then do wear protective goggles. It only takes one flying piece of metal or a stone for you to lose your eyesight.

Vision

Most children have perfect 50:50 vision. But as we grow our vision may change and fall into one of three main categories, all of which can be corrected by wearing glasses or contact lenses. Some people don't see all colors.

Short-sightedness is common. You can see things that are close up but have difficulty seeing things clearly in the distance.

Long-sightedness happens from about the age of 40 until about 60 when the eyesight tends toward short-sightedness again.

Astigmatism is when the cornea, the covering of the eye is not perfectly cylindrical (round). This causes problems particularly at night and in low light. Sufferers complain of blurred images.

Glasses and Contact Lenses

Both glasses and contact lenses are used to correct vision. Glasses do it more accurately and can give almost perfect sight. However, contact lenses vary in their effectiveness. They can be hard or soft. Hard lenses are more difficult to tolerate and it can take several weeks to adjust to them. Soft lenses can be tolerated easily and cause less irritation. But soft lenses are more likely to cause infections, and they tear easily. When not in the eye contact lenses must be kept sterile and rinsed before use. You should wash your hands before inserting or removing them. Both types are easy to lose. I know because I'm always losing mine! Disposable lenses are also available. Your optician will advise you about which type is best for you.

Eye Tests

If you can't see clearly to do whatever you want to do, you should go for an eye test. They only take about half an hour and are quite fun. To check your vision, each eye is covered in turn as you try to read charts with different sized letters on them. The optician also checks the general health of the eye by looking for any cuts or abrasions on its surface, or any infections. They then do a fundoscopy by shining a light into the eye and looking through a lens to see the retina (at the back of the inside of the eye) which is covered in blood vessels. This examination tells the optician (and doctors) many things, such as whether a person has high blood pressure, diabetes, or even certain infections.

You should have regular eye check-ups. In certain countries, if you work using a computer all day your employer has, by law, to provide eye tests free of charge.

Damaging Eyesight: We can ruin our eyesight if we spend too much time staring at computer screens, playing computer games, using the Internet, working, etc. It's very important to take breaks from looking at a computer screen. Look up every now and again and focus your eyes on something further away. Take a few minutes break every 20 minutes and take a proper break every hour to save your eyesight.

The Most Common Eye Infection is conjunctivitis. The eye becomes red and itchy, and weeps. The two main causes are viruses and bacteria which are very contagious (passed on by contact). If you have conjunctivitis, always wash your hands before and after touching your eyes. It should be treated with an antibiotic cream or drops as soon as possible.

Does everyone fart?

Farting is natural. Everybody farts. It is the body's way of expelling the gases that form as food is broken down during the digestive process. Evidence suggests that holding this wind in can be harmful and may eventually cause your bowel to stop working properly. As they say, it's better out than in!

FADS AND CRAZES

What's hip and happening today will be well out of date by the time this book is published. Crazes happen! Whatever it is, you can bet your bottom dollar that everyone will want it and in just a few weeks it will be forgotten and there'll be a new craze. There's nothing wrong with crazes. In fact, they're often fun but they can be expensive. If you spend all your money every other week on the latest fad you'll end up broke and with closets full of unfashionable junk! Sometimes it's better to spend your money on something *you* really want. Besides, you can always borrow someone else's latest fad!

Sometimes girls get bullied for not joining in with the latest craze or not having the latest *in* stuff but that's no reason to succumb. If you're confident about who you are and what you want then you can ignore any teasing or bullying. Bullying is a sign of weakness (the bully's). It's a sign of strength to do what *you* want rather than follow the crowd.

FARTING

Not only is it natural to fart but for some mad reason it causes endless hilarity among boys. Flammable gas is expelled during farting and can be set alight. Boys love that! But as you've no doubt been told all your life, playing with fire is not a good idea. See **Wind**.

FAT

There's more pressure than ever before to look slim and lose weight, even if you're not fat. There's a *huge* difference between being a normal size and being fat. Some girls seem to think if they're not as skinny as a supermodel they are fat. Wrong!

Everyone has a different body shape. Some girls are bigger than others (not fatter – *bigger!*). They are built differently and literally have bigger bones! No amount of dieting will ever make a girl like this look like a supermodel. Because of their genetic make up some girls can eat and eat and do no exercise and never put on weight; while others eat like a frightened rabbit, exercise until they drop and still put on weight! And that can be soul destroying. But you can't change your genetic make up. You are what you are so you may as well enjoy yourself, unless of course you *want* to be miserable for years.

OK, here's the deal. Food is energy. We need food to live but if you eat too much the body cleverly stores it away as fat to use later. Now, the rate this happens depends on your physical make up. But the basic rules apply.

- **Overeating will make you fat.**
- **Doing little or no exercise will make you fat.**
- **Eating too much of the wrong foods will make you fat.**
- **Crash diets only work while you keep to them *and* they can cause deficiencies of certain essential nutrients and be very dangerous. When you stop a diet you put on weight again.**
- **The only answer is to eat a balanced and healthy diet for the rest of your life; and exercise regularly.**

There are medical conditions that can make you fat but they only affect a very small minority of girls. Often the real problem is not using your willpower to control what you eat. If you eat a healthy diet and exercise most of the time then perhaps one day you feel depressed so you eat three chocolate bars. Well, that little lapse of concentration amounts to 750 calories. To give you an idea of what that means: a 15-minute *brisk* walk will work off the calories from *one* slice of bread and butter. A run for an hour at a brisk pace may just about work off three bars of chocolate. It's not easy to work off calories so if weight is a problem for you, always be careful about what you eat. The best way to keep your appropriate body weight and be healthy is to eat a balanced diet and to do regular exercise such as running, skipping, swimming, dancing, etc. See **Food and Nutrition**, **Willpower**.

> ***Slim* does not necessarily mean *healthy*.**
> **Life is for living and enjoying;**
> **not to be a punishment!**

FEELINGS
See **Anger, Happiness, Jealousy,** and **Love**.

FEVER
Fever means having a high temperature. The normal body temperature is a tightly controlled 37°C and if it rises even to 37.5°C it is called having a temperature. A high temperature is 38°C plus. If we get too hot or too cold we die.

A fever is the body's response to infection or inflammation. The most likely cause is a viral or bacterial infection. A teenage girl with a temperature could have anything from tonsillitis to meningitis to pneumonia. A temperature is a warning sign and must be considered with other symptoms in order to diagnose the cause. If you have a fever and other symptoms for more than 1-2 days you should seek medical help urgently. Meningitis has recently caused the death of a number of children and students, so it would be wise to know the symptoms. See **Meningitis.**

FIND OUT FOR YOURSELF
All doctors take the Hippocratic oath by which they promise to do the best for their patients. They won't intentionally do anything to harm them. Almost all doctors care very deeply for their patients and any treatment they embark on will be intended to benefit the

patient. However, mistakes can happen; doctors are human after all. The doctor-patient relationship is based on *trust* and *consent*. As a patient, it's up to you to consent to a treatment or to taking a medicine. As with any decision about your body it's as well to know what you are consenting to. Before you take any pills or have treatment ask your doctor: *What will the pills do? Do I really need them (or it)? Would I get well anyway, even if I don't take them (or have the treatment)? What are the side effects? Have you done this operation before?*

If you have a medical condition then find out as much as you can about it from books, the Internet, support groups, government agencies (see phone directories and the list at the end of this book). Your doctor may also be able to give you a fact sheet or advise where you can find out more. Understanding your illness will make it far easier to cope with and to make decisions about your treatment. This applies to both conventional *and* alternative medicine. Apply your common sense before you embark on any treatment.

FINGERNAILS

Long, strong elegant fingernails are what most girls want. Your genetic inheritance, good food, and willpower can all help you have them. Nails grow from a nail bed at a rate of about half an inch (1cm) every three months. *Not fast enough!* I hear you cry. It takes about six months to grow a whole fingernail and about a year and a half to grow a toe nail.

Biting your nails can transfer germs to your mouth, and also cause infections to develop around your fingernails. It can also disrupt the nail bed and the nails may not grow properly. Many diseases affect the nails and close inspection indicates to a doctor the presence of conditions such as anemia, fungal infections, psoriasis (a skin condition), and thyroid disease.

> **Brown Nails:** Commonly caused by cigarette smoking.
>
> **Yellow Nails:** Indicate psoriasis and fungal infections.
>
> **Small white spots:** These are normal and are caused by air pockets during nail growth *not* a deficiency of calcium.

The strength of your nails is due to the structure of the keratin you produce and this is in part genetic. There are various lotions available which are claimed to strengthen nails and some are better than others.

The cuticle is the bit of skin that joins the finger to the nail. In cold weather it can become hard and scaly, so keep the skin well moisturized during winter.

Infection of the skin around the nail: The skin becomes red, swollen and tender as pus accumulates under it. The nail may be discolored. The infection is caused by bacteria and if caught early can be treated with antibiotics. If not treated the pus may need to be surgically removed by a doctor, after which a course of antibiotics is needed. This type of bacterial infection is more likely if you bite your nails.

See **Antisocial Habits.**

FIRST AID

Knowing how to give first aid can save lives. It's important that everyone knows what to do (and what *not* to do) in a medical emergency (such as an accident, sports injury, or heart attack) until the professionals arrive to take over. I hope you will do a First Aid course. They are run by organizations such the Red Cross. Find your nearest first aid organization in the local phone directory or ask your doctor or at your local library. Sign up and get yourself trained.

FLU (INFLUENZA) AND COLDS

People often say they have the flu when what they actually have is a head cold. So, what's the difference? Both flu and colds are caused by viruses and there is no medical cure for either.

COLDS are caused by over 300 different viruses, which is why you never become immune to catching colds. Your immune system fights off one cold bug only to find hundreds more that your body doesn't recognize are lining up to get you.

The symptoms of a cold center around your head and include: *blocked or runny nose, a slight temperature, sneezing, headaches, and tiredness.*

FLU affects your whole body and symptoms include: *high temperature, shivering, all-over aching feeling, headache, and a dry cough.*

Every year, usually in winter, a different strain of flu virus strikes. We feel really dreadful for a couple of days but soon recover.

You catch flu by inhaling or ingesting little droplets in the air or on your hands from someone who has sneezed or coughed while having the flu. These little droplets can easily be transferred from your hands to your mouth. People with long-term illnesses, such as diabetes, asthma, cystic fibrosis, heart and kidney disease should have a flu injection to protect them.

To help you to avoid getting colds and flu, always wash your hands *before* eating. You do not need to go to a doctor with a cold or flu (but see **Meningitis** which has similar but worse and more symptoms).

If you have a cold or the flu, rest in bed and sleep it off, drink lots of liquid (especially water), take a painkiller if necessary but read the instructions carefully and don't take any more than is recommended for your age.

See **Antibiotics**.

FOOD AND NUTRITION

You don't need me to tell you food is fabulous. Ask a group of friends what their favorite food is, then stand back and watch them drool as they start talking about their grandmother's dreamy chocolate cake or hot crispy french fries . . .

Good Enough to Eat

If you're lucky, someone in your house will be a great cook and you will already know about delicious food and how to make it. If not, try some of the tantalizing recipes given in books, magazines, newspapers, and on TV cooking shows. Be adventurous, try things you've never had before. Most people teach themselves to cook. Anyone can do it, so have a go. Find a book that gives you basic information about cooking. Have it, or a dictionary, by you in case you come across any specialist terms for the first time, such as *baste* the meat, or heat the sauce in a double boiler.

Good Bugs versus Bad Bugs

As a teenager, you'll probably grab some quick meals away from home. Be a bit careful because bugs (bacteria) multiply in food that is kept warm for hours rather than kept *piping hot*. If you're given a piece of food that is *just warm*, ask for it to be reheated. And don't eat *meat* sandwiches if they've been sitting around somewhere warm for hours. Instead, go for an all-vegetable filling. Our bodies are full of both good and bad bugs but we stay well as long as the good bugs are kept strong and healthy, and we don't overload the system by taking in too many bad bugs.

Why eat boring food when even simple easy-to-prepare dishes can be made mouth-wateringly delicious? Homemade food made with fresh ingredients may take longer to make than a pre-prepared meal in a tin-foil packet but it will be far more delicious and much better for you. Making food look and smell irresistible is all part of the fun. Use the brilliant oranges, reds, greens, purples of fresh glistening vegetables to please your eye as well as tempt your taste buds.

The adults in your life would probably be delighted if you took charge of cooking one meal a week. And when you cook, make it a pleasure for everyone. Eating with your friends or family is often the one time of day when you get a chance to talk to one another.

You Are What You Eat

The sure way to have a good clear-thinking brain, glossy hair, good teeth, clear skin, a good body-weight for your build, loads of energy, and a long and *healthy* life is to eat a balanced diet and drink plenty of water.

What is a Balanced Diet?

Your body is a miraculous powerhouse of biochemical activity. Its fuel is food. Your energy comes from the food you eat, and every cell in your body needs water to perform its work. Not many of us are lucky enough to live on recently-cropped food that we have grown or reared ourselves. But we can try to eat foods that are as fresh and natural as possible to obtain the carbohydrates, proteins, and fats that our bodies need. Don't ever waste your time fussing about the percentage of different foods you eat. As long as the kitchen cupboards and fridge are regularly stocked up with foods that include fruit, vegetables, grains, bread, pasta, meat, fish, eggs, butter, and vegetable oils, and you eat a fair mix of them all over a week, you will get what you need. Over any one week, an ideal balanced diet would include: *vegetables and fruits* (to make up roughly 50 percent of your food intake); grains (about 35 percent); and protein (about 15 percent).

See also **Water.**

Vegetables and Fruits: Eat plenty of raw and dried fruit and a variety of raw or cooked vegetables. An easy way of ensuring you get a good mix of the nutrients you need is to include vegetables of different colors: dark and light green, yellow, white (e.g. potatoes), orange, and red.

Dried fruits are a concentrated source of sweetness and other nutrients that are far better for you than chocolates and sweets which are loaded with refined sugar as well as artificial additives and coloring to which some people are allergic.

Whole grains contain more essential nutrients and fiber than grains that have been dehusked (like white rice and flour). Whole grains include wheat, barley, rye, corn, brown or wild rice, millet, and buckwheat. These are available as whole grains and flours in health food stores and many supermarkets, and are the basic ingredient of a wonderful variety of delicious breads, pastas, and cakes. Try them all. There are plenty of vegetarian recipe books full of tasty recipes if you want to cook whole grains.

Proteins: Meat and fish are excellent sources of protein but they are not the only ones. Other foods with a high protein content include beans, soybean products, lentils, and nuts.

Animal protein is harder for your body to break down and digest than vegetable protein. However, in dairy products such as yogurt and cheese the enzymes used in the manufacturing process have already partially digested the proteins and calcium, which makes them easier for you to absorb.

Food Groups: It gets boring to worry about what and how much of anything you're popping into your mouth. Eat what and as much as you instinctively enjoy. If you feel energetic, clear-headed, and healthy, you sleep well, and are neither too fat nor too thin, you'll probably be getting it about right for you. If you don't feel fit, try adjusting the balance of your food intake. It won't be the same for everyone so experiment for yourself. Your food intake needs to include about 60-70 percent carbohydrates, 20-25 percent protein; and 10-15 percent fat. Some foods are the major source of one of them while others contain a mixture of them.

Sources of Carbohydrates, Protein, and Fat

Food Group	Found in:
Protein	Poultry; white fish without its skin; eggs; *low-fat* yogurts and dairy products such as milk, cheese, and butter.
Protein and fat	Meat; cheese; yogurt; milk; cream; ice-cream; oily fish; and fish with its skin.
Protein and carbohydrate	Soy (soya) bean products; lentils; beans; and seeds such as pumpkin, sesame, linseed, and sunflower.
Carbohydrates	Grains, cereals, pasta; bread; potatoes; fruits; most vegetables; sugars including fruit sugars, honey, and maple syrup.
Carbohydrates and fat	Avocado; French fries; crisps or chips; biscuits or cookies; cakes; and sauces.
Fats	Olive, sunflower, safflower, and other vegetable oils (preferably organic); butter; margarines and other vegetable oil spreads.
Protein, fats and carbohydrates	Nuts; all whole grains.

Other Food Facts

Fiber, the body's broom, contains a lot of cellulose which our digestive system is not good at breaking down. It travels through the gut like a sponge mopping up toxins, excess fats, and cholesterol. It keeps waste matter moving through your body, cleaning up the walls of your intestines and bowels along the way.

Fiber is to be found in all vegetables; fruit; whole grains such as brown rice; nuts, and seeds; wholemeal and wheat breads, cereals, and pastas. Every day, eat some of these, or products made with them, and you'll be getting enough fiber.

Pumpkin and sunflower seeds supply essential fatty acids *and* clean up your insides.

Some fats are good for you but too much of any of them is not. Fats that our body can utilize are *essential* to enable us to store the fat-related vitamins we need.

Cholesterol is a steroid not a fat. An *excess* of cholesterol in the body may cause congestion in the blood-carrying arteries but, also, it is *essential* to the manufacture of hormones from the adrenal and sex glands, vitamin D, and bile acid, all of which are vital to life. If you're eating a healthy balanced diet, don't worry about cholesterol.

Calcium builds strong bones and teeth. It is important to drink milk because your bones need calcium when they are growing. Try also to eat plenty of the other foods that contain it in a form that is more easily absorbed by the body: yogurt, fish, meat, poultry, most dark green vegetables, sesame seeds, nuts especially almonds, and soy products such as tofu. It's important to eat some of these foods regularly. If your calcium levels are high while your bones are forming you'll have a better chance of *not* getting osteoporosis (thinning of the bones) when you're an old lady. Some quite young girls have begun to get osteoporosis, perhaps because they are drinking only skimmed milk.

Salt is found in most of the food we eat. We need its sodium, but too much salt is not good for us. Try not to add extra salt to your food. Your body will soon adjust and your food will taste just as good without it.

Sugar makes you fat when it is refined (separated) from its source (where it occurs naturally in combination with other nutrients). Because sugar, in the form of glucose or fructose (fruit sugar), is found in fruits and vegetables combined with other nutrients, your body takes time to break it down and release its energy to you. And that's good.

Refined sugar added to your food gives you a quick energy boost but, without the combination of nutrients that are found in fruits and vegetables, your blood sugar level quickly plummets and the sugar is stored as fat.

Sugar when it is a natural part of a *whole* food is good for you. But an excess of *refined* sugars can cause fat, fatigue, depression, irritability, muscle weakness, headaches, shakiness, asthma, diabetes, and hardening of the arteries. Phew! I'm scaring myself.

Like most of us you probably got hooked on refined sugar when you were little. You're going to have to work hard at it but keep trying to reduce the number of spoonfuls of refined sugar you stir into or sprinkle over the food you eat. You'll soon find yourself discovering an infinite variety of real and delicious food tastes; and gagging on anything that has been overly sweetened with refined sugar.

Foods you'd be better off without

The only *dieting* a relatively healthy girl should ever do is to cut out foods that prevent her body functioning efficiently. This includes sweets, candies, chocolates, refined sugars and artificial sweeteners, drinks containing caffeine (coffee, tea, alcohol, some fizzy drinks), deep-fat fried foods, and hydrogenated fats. This is not to say you should *never* eat these things, just don't gorge on them to the point where you don't feel like eating a good balance of healthy foods.

Cutting out fats will *not* make you thin; your body needs some fats. Eating a balanced diet that includes about 50 percent fruit and vegetables, some protein and fat, and drinking at least 6-8 glasses of water a day, is the best way to restore the natural balance and weight of your body and is far more enjoyable than counting calories.

Who Eats What?

A balanced diet is the easiest and surest way for us to take in all the nutrients we need to stay alive and healthy. Vegetarians and vegans have to work a bit harder to get what they need. If you choose to become one, then do please get yourself some specialist books from the library or leaflets from a vegetarian or vegan society. Study them carefully so you understand the subject fully *before* you start.

Omnivores have the choice of every kind of yummy food there is. Being an omnivore is the easiest way to obtain a balanced diet because meat and fish provide complete proteins. You don't have to eat meat or fish every day; 2 or 3 times a week is plenty.

Vegetarians eat everything *except* meat or fish. You may choose to become vegetarian because you don't like the taste of meat or fish; or because you don't like the thought of animals being killed. However, meat and fish supply us with essential proteins and other vital nutrients. Eggs, nuts, soy (soya) products, and dairy products such as milk, cheese, yogurt, ice-cream, and butter also supply protein.

You can be perfectly healthy living on a vegetarian diet but you *must* get some informative books about it and make sure you understand fully what it involves *before* you start.

Vegans do *not* eat meat, fish, or any animal produce such as eggs, milk, butter, cheese or any food that contains them. Simply *not* eating these foods would cause deficiencies in your body, which is not a good idea for a growing girl. To be a vegan *and* remain healthy requires plenty of time dedicated to preparing beans, pulses, and lentils. Only specific mixtures of these and grains make up complete proteins which is what you need, as well as tofu (soybean curd) and some vitamin pills, every week. Meat, eggs, and dairy products are the main sources of vitamin B_{12}. If you get your protein *only* from vegetables, you need to take a B_{12} supplement. If, when you're older, the vegan way of eating appeals to you, get some informative books and study it fully *before* you start.

Is it hard being a vegetarian?

Not at all! Once you've learned the basics, find some books with tasty sounding recipes and start experimenting. Supermarkets sell most of the ingredients you need but you may need to go to a health food store for some things. Most restaurants include vegetarian dishes on their menu. Even meat eaters eat a lot of vegetarian food, such as baked beans, baked potato with cheese, salads, and *ratatouille* (find that in a recipe book; it's easy to make and scrumptious either hot or cold).

As you can see, food and nutrition is a huge and fascinating subject that we have only begun to look at in this book. It's up to you now to find out more, and to discover delicious recipes. Don't ever panic about food, just make sure it looks and tastes good to you. If you get really interested in it you may even decide you want to make it your career. You could become a chef, open a restaurant or café; study nutrition and become a dietitian advising

Dr. Dave's Top Tips – Food

Food is great, give yourself time to enjoy it, and relax for at least 10 minutes after a big meal before you get on with doing anything too strenuous, like the washing-up!

Eat fresh vegetables (raw or cooked) and some fruit every day, preferably organically grown. Wash and dry them before preparing or eating them.

Use organic ingredients (food grown without artificial fertilizers and pesticides) whenever possible.

Choose to eat whole grains such as brown rice, and wholemeal or wheat breads.

Use organic oils whenever possible. Olive oil is best to cook with as it can be heated to higher temperatures without becoming harmful. Other oils are great for salad dressings but when heated they are not as good for you.

Lightly steamed (rather than boiled) vegetables taste better and retain more of their water-soluble vitamins. Use the vitamin-rich vegetable water to flavor sauces and gravies.

Eat butter (thinly spread) rather than *hydrogenated* margarine which has a molecular structure that our body does not know how to process.

Start and end each day with a glass of plain water. And drink 6-8 glasses throughout each day.

For every fizzy drink, cup of tea or coffee, or glass of alcohol, drink a glass of water as well.

Reduce the amount of refined sugars, candies and sweets you eat. Never use artificial sweeteners.

To prevent bacteria on raw meat contaminating other food, keep a special board on which only meat is prepared. Wash your hands thoroughly after handling raw meat.

If you've just cut meat, don't use the same knife to cut vegetables or fruit. Wash it well under hot water first.

Never eat meat that is not well cooked, i.e. it should have no pink bits at the center and the juices should run clear. At home, using a meat thermometer will tell you when the internal temperature is high enough to destroy bacteria.

Store meat in the fridge as soon as possible after buying it. Bacteria don't like the cold.

Refrigerate all vegetables as soon as possible to retain their natural sweetness. Enzymes gobble up the natural sugars if vegetables are stored at room temperature.

Try to buy fresh-looking vegetables that are stored in cool conditions rather than limp ones that have been sitting around in the sun for hours.

As soon as any leftover cooked food is cool, put it in the fridge to prevent bacteria growing.

Cook eggs well to destroy any salmonella bugs that may be lurking in them and which cause food poisoning.

After washing up, rinse the residue of detergent off dishes and utensils and let them drain dry rather than dry them with a bacteria-harboring cloth.

hospital or private patients, or a research scientist, or a health inspector checking that food for the public is prepared in hygienic conditions; become a TV presenter, a journalist, or author specializing in cooking or health and food matters; become a caterer for lavish dinner parties and wedding banquets. Or you may just want to feed yourself and your family delicious and healthy food.

FRECKLES

Freckles are simply tiny patches of skin where there is naturally more pigment. You can't get rid of them and why would you want to, they're very attractive. Freckles can appear after exposure to the sun.

FRIENDS

Most of us know how awful it feels when our best buddy suddenly dumps us for no apparent reason and starts going around with someone else. Suddenly there's no one to talk to, or to share secrets and hang out with in school.

Friends are hugely important. They help us work out who we are by sharing our experiences and helping us make sense of them. They support us when we're down and have fun with us when everything's great. Girlfriends are especially important and a good friendship may last all your life. Friendship should work both ways. If you're loyal and caring about your friends they will come to love and trust you and be loyal and caring in return. Try always to make time for them – see they're OK. Listen to them as well as talking about yourself.

I used to think I should try and *make* friends like me. Now, I know if I just be myself, they will. If a friend sticks with you through thick and thin and likes you for what you are then she (or he) is a real friend. If they don't they aren't worth bothering with. What good is a friend who disappears whenever you need her? That said, some people can only be what they are and you may find you can appreciate some friends for the ways they *are* good for you, even though there may be times when they simply can't give you what you need.

As you start having boyfriends it's easy to lose touch with your other friends. Try to avoid that, even if the best you can do is an occasional chat on the phone to let them know you haven't forgotten them. Boyfriends will come and go but real friends will last and should be valued.

Not all boys fancy every girl and vice versa so you can still have good friends who are boys without them becoming *boyfriends*. Sometimes it's a lot easier being really good friends without all the emotional stuff that goes with having a full-on relationship. But it can be difficult if one of you suddenly starts to be attracted to the other. For some reason this attraction can make us act very oddly. We may become shy, say things we don't mean, or be rude without meaning to. If the attraction is not mutual then, sadly, it may end a beautiful friendship! At this point you'll need your girl friends.

FUNGAL INFECTIONS

Fungi are badly named. They are *not* fun guys! Fungal infections are often just irritating nuisances but some can be worse than that. Your doctor or pharmacist can easily identify them for you. Here's a few to look out for.

Athlete's foot can affect anyone, not just athletes. Fungi love dark, damp, wet, and warm places, so they really love the sweltering atmosphere inside gym shoes, particularly between your fourth and fifth toes. They start with a red itchy rash, followed by cracked and weeping skin which can be painful.

Prevention is always better than cure. So, *wash and dry your feet well*, especially between the toes, then dust with talcum powder to help keep them dry. *Only wear wool or cotton socks* and avoid socks made from man-made fibers. *Wear sandals* when it's hot and *never* wear anyone else's shoes or socks. *Wear protective shoes or socks* in swimming pool changing rooms to avoid picking up or spreading a fungal infection. Like goggles, they are available at most public swimming pools. Treatment is with an antifungal cream available from a pharmacist. Use it sparingly. Read and follow the instructions.

Body rash (pale patches): A common fungal infection is something called *Pityriasis versicolor*. Small patches of surface skin lose their color or pigment. They're more noticeable if you have a tan and are very visible on dark skin. It's easily treated with an antifungal shampoo that contains selenium but you must keep up the treatment for six weeks.

Nail infections are very unpleasant and difficult to treat. The nail thickens and changes color. Treatment is with antifungal pills which you swallow and may have to keep taking for months before it clears up.

Ringworm causes circular scaly lesions which start to clear up from the middle while spreading like ripples in a pond outward from the center. This condition is most common in children and the fungus is easily caught from pets or farm animals. It also can be treated with antifungal creams.

Thrush is caused by a *yeast* called Candida Albicans. See **Candida Albicans**, and **Thrush**.

Why is glandular fever called the kissing disease?

Because the virus that causes it is spread in saliva, one sure way to get it is to kiss someone who has it!

GAS FIRES: CARBON MONOXIDE POISONING

Every year, too many young people (often students in cheap accommodation or kids left alone on holiday) die of carbon monoxide poisoning from gas appliances. You can't see, taste, or even smell carbon monoxide but it can kill you within hours. You are particularly vulnerable when asleep.

The symptoms are very like having a viral infection: tiredness, drowsiness, headache, nausea, and pains in the chest and stomach. Carbon monoxide poisoning sneaks up on you and can affect your mental capacity without you knowing it. Sudden exertion can cause collapse. If you or anyone in your house has such symptoms, switch off the gas appliance, open a window to let air circulate. Call a doctor or emergency services immediately. Describe symptoms and tell them you suspect carbon monoxide poisoning.

Keep Warm *and* Stay Alive

A properly installed and maintained gas appliance is perfectly safe. But when gas does not burn properly, excess toxic carbon monoxide is produced. If you live in, or are about to move into, rented accommodation, your landlord must by law provide you with written proof that annual safety checks have been carried out by an accredited gas engineer. Ask to see it.

NEVER use a gas appliance if the flame burns yellow or orange; nor if there are soot stains on or around the appliance, or if the pilot light frequently blows out, or if there is condensation in the room in which the gas appliance is installed.

NEVER cover an appliance or block the air vents.

NEVER block or obstruct any fixed ventilation grilles or air bricks.

NEVER block or cover outside flues.

DO leave a window partly open to let air circulate. You may need to fit a window lock to prevent the window being opened wide enough for an intruder to get in.

GAY RELATIONSHIPS

When people of the same sex are only sexually attracted to people of the same sex as themselves they are currently known as being *gay*. Men who only love men are homosexual; women who only love other women are homosexual and known as lesbians; and any one who is attracted to both males and females is bi-sexual. They all experience the same range of feelings toward their partners as heterosexual (male/female) couples.

GENITALS

Fetuses are physically the same when they start life in the womb. But under the influence of hormones the genital tissues develop to be either male or female.

Girl babies develop a vagina leading to the cervix (opening of the uterus). Surrounding the vaginal entrance and urethra (exit for urine) are labia which have inner and outer lips. The outer lips lap over the clitoris (at the front of the genitals) and extend right back to just in front of the anus. As girls mature, pubic hair grows on the outer labia. The inner labia join up at the front to form a fleshy lump called the clitoris. The inner lips are thinner than the outer ones and they surround the vagina. When a woman is sexually aroused, the clitoris hardens and becomes sensitive to touch during love-making. Stimulation of the clitoris can bring a woman to orgasm (sexual climax).

Female genitalia are very close to the anus so it's important to wash daily. After using the toilet, wipe yourself from front to back to avoid the spread of bacteria from the anus to the vagina.

A boy baby's genital tissue develops into a penis, and two testicles which are contained within a scrotum sack which hangs outside the body. The penis has two functions: it's used to pee with and for having sex. When a man becomes sexually aroused, the penis becomes hard (erect) and closes off the bladder so he can't pee during sex. Like the female clitoris, stimulation of the penis excites and brings a man to his sexual climax during which he ejaculates semen containing millions of sperm. If a man is not wearing a condom and this ejaculation is into (or close to) a woman's vagina at a time when she is fertile, then she is very likely to become pregnant.

All boys are born with a foreskin, a flexible sleeve of skin that surrounds the penis. It is often surgically removed for religious or medical reasons in an operation called circumcision when the boy is a baby. A man's ability to have and enjoy sex does not depend on having a foreskin.

Testicles are enclosed in the scrotum to hold them outside the body where it is cooler than the rest of the body so sperm can be made in them. Sperm are destroyed if the scrotum gets too hot.

When a boy is cold, the muscles of the scrotum contract, pulling the testicles closer to the body to keep them warm.

GLANDULAR FEVER (KISSING DISEASE)

Its real name is infectious mononucleosis. You can catch it from *kissing* someone who is infected. It's caused by a virus called Epstein Barr and is common in young adults. The virus attacks the immune system and causes symptoms such as: *sore throat, fever, swollen glands, chronic tiredness, and an enlarged liver.*

Diagnosis is difficult and relies on a blood test to confirm the presence of the virus. But the virus isn't always easy to isolate.

For months after the acute stage of glandular fever, a person can feel lethargic – completely lacking any energy.

Treatment is supportive which means you must rest, often in bed; drink plenty of fluids (especially water) and eat healthily. It's a variable illness and some people recover much quicker than others. It's best to do as much as you can and rest when you feel tired ... Oh, and don't pass it on by KISSING anyone!

GLASSES

People used to get teased about wearing glasses but specs are now fun, fashionable, and come in a range of designer frames (with a price to match!). So, if you've been prescribed glasses, get out there and wear them with pride. Not only will they improve your eyesight, you may also be extra attractive in them because a lot of boys think they're very sexy! See also **Eyes.**

GROWING PAINS

Some teenagers experience aches and pains as they go through puberty. During this rapid growth phase, the hormone responsible for it, funnily enough, is called *growth hormone.* It is released at night when you're asleep. It is normal for a teenager to have mild aches and pains in her arms, legs, or shoulders but if they are severe see your doctor.

GUILT

You can feel just as guilty for *not* doing or saying what you know you should have, as for doing something you shouldn't have done. Lying to your parents about where you've been; or perhaps kissing your best friend's boyfriend are both certain to produce some fairly gut-wrenching feelings of guilt! You probably knew when you were doing it that you shouldn't, but at the time you really wanted to so you did! But, how do you put it right? The best way is to admit what you've done, apologize, and try to make clear how it happened, that you didn't mean it to, and that you will endeavor not to repeat it. Even if it's hard to do it, if you clear the air in this way as soon as possible you won't have to live in fear of being found out and you can face your friend (or whoever) in the future knowing you've been honest with them. Gradually, you'll know when to avoid doing what makes you feel guilty. It's a lot less troublesome!

HAPPINESS

If you are happy you're likely to work harder, do better, and have more fun. Most of us feel reasonably happy most of the time and extremely happy some of the time; with periods of anxiety, boredom, sadness, excitement, loneliness, detachment, etc., all thrown in at different times. If you can consistently work out and choose to do what feels right for *you*, you've got a better chance of being happy a lot of the time and achieving what you want. And sometimes, such as when you do something fantastic, you will feel overwhelmingly, marvelously happy. Try to let happiness come from inside yourself rather than depending on someone else for it. For example, girls often say *if only so-and-so loved me, I would be happy.* Whereas, if you are happy within yourself, you will survive perfectly well if he doesn't. And with the pressure off, that special person may be more likely to love you anyway!

HAIR

That stuff on your head is just dead protein! But what you do with it can make a fantastic difference to the way you look and feel. Whatever style you go for, looking after your hair is simple. All it *needs* is to be cut in the style of your choice and washed regularly. Cheap shampoos and conditioners are just as good as expensive ones!

Student Days

When I was a student living with some friends, one of the girls was convinced if she didn't wash her hair for three months it would revert to its natural state! She claimed shampoos get rid of the hair's natural oils. Well, that may be true but my advice is don't try it! Her hair became so smelly and horrible that the rest of us just had to wash her hair for her! The three-month theory maybe OK if you live on a desert island but most of us live in areas with high pollution and grime, and our scalp sweats. No doubt about it, regular shampooing is essential!

HEADACHES

Many teenagers get headaches. Most are caused by *tension* and it doesn't help to worry about them! The pain is usually felt like a tight band around both sides of the head and often builds up in the evening. They usually get better on their own. When you feel your head becoming tense, you can probably help yourself by recognizing the signs and trying to relax. If you can, take a break to distract you from whatever is worrying you. Hormone fluctuations during menstruation can also cause headaches. Another form of headache is a *cluster* headache in which a stabbing pain centers behind one eye which can become bloodshot and water. They occur in clusters of three or four headaches a day over a few days and may recur a few months apart. None of these headaches are usually a cause for concern.

Migraine headaches can be very debilitating and are said to be the worst kind of headache you can have. They tend to follow a pattern, starting with an AURA (problems seeing) followed 10-60 minutes later by a throbbing one-sided headache, nausea, and vomiting.

Certain things can trigger attacks in susceptible people, such as cheese, chocolate, anxiety, exercise, and travel. Pills can be taken to prevent a migraine and medication is available to treat an attack once it starts. Rather than growing out of them people learn to avoid the triggers and control the onset of symptoms.

When to See the Doctor:

There can be serious causes of headaches, such as meningitis, but they will be accompanied by other symptoms. If headaches persist or you have other symptoms such as fever, stiff neck, and difficulty looking at light, or they get worse when you cough, sneeze, or bend your head, you should see a doctor urgently.

HEART

No wonder the heart has become the symbol of love, without it pumping away we couldn't live to fall in love. It beats 110,880 times a day and thumps extra hard with excitement when your true love comes near.

Children rarely get heart disease so why am I about to tell you about it? Well, half of everyone you know will probably die of heart disease later in life unless we do something about it *now*. The key to preventing heart disease is not to build up fatty material in your arteries. It starts to build up when you're as young as twelve! So, to live to a ripe old age: *don't smoke* (this makes a huge difference); *eat healthily* (some fat is OK but don't live on chips); *do some **fun** exercise* such as rollerblading, disco dancing, aerobics, whatever you enjoy! See **Exercise; Food and Nutrition: What is a Balanced Diet?;** and **Smoking**.

HELP!

If you're in trouble don't keep it to yourself. Whatever it is and however much you feel you can't tell anyone, never suffer in silence or your problem may only get worse. That is true of anything, from being attacked, bullied, depressed, or ill. That old saying, *a problem shared is a problem halved* is true. Talking to someone will begin to relieve your bottled-up tension and having got it out into the open there will then be two heads to find a solution, not just one! Talk to a responsible and caring adult who you know you can trust. That may be a friend, a parent, a teacher, a doctor, a specialist support group or child helpline. See **Support Groups**.

HEPATITIS

This is literally inflammation of the liver and there are different types. The main ones are:

Hepatitis A is caused by a virus that is spread by eating food such as uncooked shellfish or food that contains fecal matter, often from the hands of people who prepare food without washing their hands after using the toilet. It causes loss of energy, nausea, joint pain, and a fever. Jaundice develops (the skin goes yellow). It also causes liver, spleen, and glands to enlarge. There's no specific treatment and it gets better on its own. It has no long term consequences.

Hepatitis B is also caused by a virus but this one is carried in infected blood, saliva, and sexual secretions. It can take six weeks to six months to incubate. It causes the same symptoms as *Hepatitis A*; but Hepatitis B can remain in the body and destroy the liver.

HIV (Human Immunodeficiency Virus)

Most kids will have heard of HIV which leads to a condition called AIDS (acquired immunodeficiency syndrome). It first became apparent among gay men but now, all over the world, **millions of males and females** are contracting HIV. It is an epidemic. After infection with the virus a person's immune system breaks down (AIDS) leaving the body unable to fight off other infections which are what ultimately lead to death.

Sadly, nowadays, when young women (and young men) decide they are ready to start having sex they *must know* that if they have sex without the man wearing a condom, they risk contracting HIV and subsequently dying. Sex is one of our most powerful urges and young women need to be aware that, although most of the young men they know will be honest and decent, there are others who would tell any lie in order to have sex. If a man tells a woman there is no need for him to wear a condom because he has never had sex before (or for any other reason), she should state very clearly:

*Nonetheless, I've made it a rule never to have sex
with any man who isn't wearing a condom.*

And stick to that until she is in a permanent relationship with
someone she knows she can trust absolutely!

**HIV is carried by an infected person in
their blood and bodily secretions, such as
saliva, tears, and semen.**

FACTS AND FICTION – HIV

HIV can be caught by:

❥ having *sexual intercourse without using a condom*
(unprotected sex).

❥ *blood transfusion and blood products.*

❥ *sharing hypodermic needles.*

❥ *using the same razor or toothbrush* as an infected person.

You *cannot* catch HIV by:

❥ *drinking from a glass* used by an infected person.

❥ *sharing towels* with an infected person.

❥ *standing next to* an infected person.

It is *unlikely* that you will catch HIV by:

❥ *tongue-kissing an infected person.* It is thought to be difficult to
transfer the virus by kissing *but* you *can* get it from a single
exposure. Be especially careful if either of you has a sore or cut
lip, gums, or tongue.

CONDOMS OFFER THE BEST PROTECTION.

HIV tests are available. If you are worried about anyone in your family, confidential HIV tests are available at specialist sexual health clinics.

See also **Aids; Contraception, Immune System; Sex**.

Am I the Only One Who Feels Like This?

Nope! Your particular combination of experiences and feelings will be unique to you but out there, somewhere, there will be many people who have had similar fears, joys, excitements, pains, depressions, loneliness; and someone will understand how you feel. So, keep looking!

IMMUNE SYSTEM

Our own immune system is our best defense against disease. When it's working well, it keeps us strong and healthy and free of infection. We come into contact with bacteria and viruses every day of our life without even being aware of our immune system destroying them. Once we've had a disease (such as measles) we make antibodies that stay in our body ready to attack immediately if we ever come into contact with it again. We become *immune to it.* Since our life depends on our immune system we should give it all the help we can, so:

- **get enough sleep.**
- **eat a regular and healthy balanced diet,** especially plenty of fresh fruit and vegetables.
- **learn how to relax** when you feel yourself becoming tense, anxious, or worried.
- **exercise regularly**.
- **drink at least 6-8 glasses of water every day.**
- **don't drink excessive amounts of alcohol.**

Some people believe that supplements such as vitamin C or zinc boosts the immune system but this has not been proven. The best way to take in nutrients is as they come *naturally combined* in fresh food.

IMMUNIZATION

The theory of immunization (vaccination, shots) is that when we are injected with a tiny amount of the dead virus of an infectious disease our body will develop antibodies to it. If we then come into contact with the virus again our antibodies will be ready to defend us from it. You should always know what sort of protection a vaccination affords. For example, cholera injections are only 50 percent effective so perhaps are not worth having, whereas others give a greater rate of protection.

If you are planning to travel, always check with your travel agent or medical adviser what vaccinations are recommended for the countries you will pass through and what the risks are. Homeopathic alternatives have not been clinically proven to give protection.

There are risks in having vaccinations so before you have one, do a bit of research at your local library, medical center, or on the

Internet to check the latest scientific findings. As always gather information, discuss it with a responsible adult, then decide for yourself whether you go ahead and have one. See **Further Reading**.

Most immunizations are given to us when we are babies but some, such as tetanus (every ten years), need to be followed up with booster injections.

Other important shots for teenagers are:

Rubella (German Measles): If contracted in early pregnancy Rubella can cause defects in the baby.

Tuberculosis (BCG): TB is spreading again in poor urban areas, such as parts of New York and London.

Dr. Dave's Top Tips to Survive Your Shots

Make sure you're healthy on the day. Postpone your appointment if you've got a cold or any other infection.

Leave at least two weeks between shots to give your body a chance to respond to each one. This will need some forethought if you're planning to travel. It's not a good idea to have *all* your shots just before you leave.

INDEPENDENCE

As a child you are dependent on your family or other responsible adults for love, care, food, a place to live, and money. Your teenage years are a process of discovering the mysteries of adult life (which most of us take a lifetime to understand) and preparing for the time when *you* will be an independent adult.

All your life, if you want to be free to choose what happens to you, to be free to walk away from any situation that is not good for you, there is one thing you are going to need and that's *money*. For your own self-respect, and to enable you to deal with anybody on an equal footing, it should be money you have earned for yourself. That way, you need be under no obligation to anyone, ever.

Believe it or not, school can help. You might think you'd rather hang out at the local donut place or down at the beach all day, talking about boys, music, clothes, and make-up. But if that's *all* you do you may eventually find it gets boring. Of course, it *is* all fascinating but it is only *part* of life. Your own self-development includes much more. What you're studying may seem irrelevant to you now but it gives you a taste of a variety of subjects from which you can work out what you're *really* interested in. Stay alert to what you *actually* find fascinating. It may be mathematics, religion, art, archaeology, music, biology experiments, sports, or teaching little children, etc. All the other girls in your class may think experiments in the laboratory or art room are deeply dull, but if they interest *you*, find out what career courses in science or art are available.

Always pursue what *you* want.

INSTINCT

Often your immediate reaction to a person or situation is instinctively correct even though you haven't apparently had time to think. We probably inherited this amazing capacity from our ancient ancestors whose strong survival instincts meant they lived long enough to produce our forebears.

Pressure is put on us all the time by people wanting us to be or do things or to act in certain ways that may not feel right to us. So, listen to your instinct. If you *feel* something is a good idea then it probably is and vice versa. If you have a bad feeling about something then it's wise not to do it. You'll be a stronger person and respected for it if you can say *no* to what you don't want, rather than just going along with everybody just to be part of the *in* crowd. It is your right to say "no" when you feel something is wrong for you.

IRRITABLE BOWEL SYNDROME (IBS)

This is usually only considered when other conditions have been ruled out. But more and more girls and young women seem to be getting irritable bowel syndrome.

Symptoms include: alternating diarrhea and constipation; abdominal pain, usually gripping but also with sharp or cutting episodes; and a bloated feeling.

Examination of the guts of these patients shows nothing – they look normal, there's no sign of inflammation, yet still their bowel is not functioning well (see **Constipation**); and nobody really knows why. It may be that many of us eat too much processed food and not enough fresh foods. So, see your doctor and keep reading whatever you can find about IBS.

Dr. Dave's Top Tips – IBS

Eat more vegetable fiber and increase the amount of fluid (especially water) you drink. See also **Food and Nutrition.**

Listen to your body: We don't listen enough to our body. If you feel you want to go to the toilet – GO!

Exercise gently: Even three lots of twenty minutes a week will help.

Some drugs are available from the pharmacist but are only useful in the short term.

J

Is jogging always good for you?

Jogging is an excellent form of exercise but too much of it can be damaging. Jogging on hard surfaces can cause shin splints (tiny fractures of the leg bones). It can also inflame soft tissues of the foot and cause knee and back problems.

JEALOUSY

The green-eyed monster! Jealousy can really get out of control, eating away at you inside, making you do things you might regret, and making you very unhappy. It can consume all your time and energy and stop you getting on with your own life. It may seem the most devastating thing in the world when the boy you love prefers somebody else but try and see it is his right to love whoever he pleases – just as it is yours – and accept it. All you can do is to try at least for part of every day to switch off the feelings. Distract yourself by doing things you really like and are interested in, especially those that require a lot of concentration. It's like taking a holiday from the pain and you can have at least a few hours a day when you're not tearing yourself apart with jealousy. The feelings will probably return the minute you stop, but in smaller chunks they are less overwhelming and bit by bit you can deal with them, put them aside each time, and gradually move on to something or someone new – and possibly better!

What are kidneys for?

We have two but only need a small amount of functioning kidney to keep alive. The kidneys filter our blood and remove waste products. The more water you drink the more dilute the urine will be; it will look almost colorless. If you drink too little water, your urine becomes concentrated and dark yellow.

KISSING

It's fab. There's no right way to kiss someone and you don't need to worry what you do with your nose! All will fit into place. There are three types of kiss: granny kissing (on the cheek); dry lip-to-lip kissing; and wet-lip or French kissing (with tongues inside one another's mouth).

If you think about it, touching someone else's lips with your own may seem weird and you can't imagine how nice it is – until you do it! It's great, but it's a very intimate thing to do so choose well who you kiss.

As with everything it's important you know when you are enjoying it and when you feel you're being forced to do more than you want. At that point you must say *I want to stop now*. Be as honest as you can about your feelings even though it is sometimes difficult. See **Assertiveness,** and **Sex**.

Oh sure, you can catch things from kissing but I don't want you to get obsessed with that. If you kiss someone with a common cold you can catch it from them. But *don't kiss* anyone with an active cold sore because you will catch the herpes virus which stays in your body forever and give you recurring cold sores for the rest of your life! Ugggh! HIV is not usually passed on by kissing but see also **HIV**.

Can head lice jump?

Head lice transfer from one person's head to another when people touch heads. Contrary to popular belief head lice can't jump! But if you're close enough to kiss someone, you're close enough to catch lice from them!

LESBIAN

A lesbian is a woman who is sexually attracted mainly to other women. It is common for teenagers to feel attracted to a member of the same sex but it doesn't necessarily mean you are a lesbian or gay. It is as if young people are discovering themselves and one another and practicing their feelings in circumstances when no sexual union is likely. However, if the feelings persist as a person gets older, then they may be gay. See **Gay Relationships**.

LICE

Lice are small blood-sucking insects which live on the human body. There are different types, named according to the part of the body they enjoy!

Head Lice seem to thrive on young schoolchildren! The adult head louse gets nice and fat feeding off the blood from a child's scalp. They lay eggs (nits) and attach them to the hairs. They also leave black bits (their droppings!) in your hair. Nits hatch into new lice. Playing games such as Chinese Whispers makes it easy for them to pass from one head to another! An itchy head can be a sign that you have nits. If one child has lice, everyone in the family should be treated. If you don't want to catch them again immediately you go back to school, all the other kids in your class need to be treated too. So, lice need to be reported to a teacher.

Treatment is with a toxic shampoo from the pharmacist. It works but some people worry about the long-term effect of using poisonous chemicals on their head.

An alternative treatment is to use the wet-combing technique. Rub conditioner into your hair to make it hard for the lice to keep their grip. Then use a very fine-toothed nit comb to scrape off all the nits. It takes a lot of patience!

Don't share towels or sleep on the same pillow as anyone who has head lice.

Pubic Lice are similar but bigger and live in the pubic hairs making the whole area very itchy. They transfer from one person to another when pubic hair touches during sex. Eggs are also laid and hatch within a week. Lice may resemble small scabs but on closer examination they move. Both the lice and the eggs must be killed, usually with a chemical called malathion.

LOVE

It can happen, some people know instantly when someone is right for them. There's still masses to learn about one another but there does seem to be some instinctive attraction between certain people. Others get to know one another as friends and then begin to realize they have fallen in love. Most people love their family but falling in love and loving someone else is different.

Like all emotions, *love* is difficult to describe. Inexplicably and overwhelmingly, you want to be with a particular boy. You love and like and care about him more than anyone else and feel really passionate about him. When you love someone, you want to share experiences with him, to be close, to know he is there for you and you for him no matter what. But, it's one thing knowing what it is and quite another knowing if what you feel is *it*! If you're *in love* with someone, you'll probably be tingling with excitement as you talk to him. You can find yourself doing things on impulse, like touching him, taking hold of his hand, or stroking his head and whispering nice things.

If you're lucky, the attraction and feelings will be mutual but, sadly, they aren't always and that can be very hard to cope with. If you've had a long relationship which breaks up it can take weeks, months, or even years to recover fully from the loss of it. Having real interests of your own, doing things you enjoy with some good girl friends will all help you to get through it. And, amazingly, you *will* meet someone else!

As a teenager you are still developing as a person. Your needs and interests will change and develop and there will be masses to discover about yourself and relationships with boys. The person you're breaking your heart over when you're 14 is unlikely to be the one you want when you are 20, 23 or 30. Not because there's anything wrong with him or you but because both of you will develop and grow in different directions. The important thing is to enjoy and genuinely feel what you feel when you feel it. It's all very fascinating and exciting!

Does everyone with meningitis die?

No they don't but it is an extremely dangerous illness and the sooner the symptoms are recognized and treated the better the chances of survival.

MASTURBATION

This means caressing your own sexual organs for pleasure. Although both girls and boys sometimes do it, boys probably do it more. And some people don't do it at all. It's not bad and does allow you to get to know your own body in private.

MENINGITIS

Never underestimate meningitis. Despite huge public awareness it remains a killer.

Meningitis is an infection of the lining of the brain and spinal cord. It can be caused by either a virus or by bacteria. It is spread by *coughing*, *sneezing*, or *kissing*. The viral type tends to be less severe and gets better on its own.§ The bacterial type is more serious and must be treated with antibiotics as soon as possible.

Meningitis spreads faster in the winter when people are more likely to be together in enclosed spaces. If an infected person coughs and sneezes, such conditions make it very easy for the bug to spread from one person to another.

Certain types of meningitis, particularly the more dangerous ones, are on the increase.

Symptoms of Meningitis

❥ **The worst headache** you've ever had.

❥ **A very high temperature.**

❥ **A stiff neck.** A good test is to see whether you can touch your chin on your chest. If you can't, see a doctor urgently.

❥ **Difficulty looking at bright lights** and it's painful to watch TV.

❥ **A rash.** The rash is different to other types of rash because it doesn't fade when you press it. The best test is to do it with a glass so you can see the rash as you press.

If you suspect you or anyone else may have meningitis, get help from a doctor *urgently*. Every minute can make the difference between life and death. It is *really* that serious!

MENSTRUATION (PERIODS)

If you didn't know about menstruation before you start having periods they would seem very frightening. But for all females, it is completely normal to bleed from the vagina once a month. As your body reaches puberty it starts a cycle of bleeding for about 4-7 days of each month. The monthly cycle of having periods usually starts when you are 12-14. It varies from girl to girl; some might start at 9 or 10, others at 15.

The blood that comes out of you is actually the tissue that lines the inside of your uterus (womb). Once a month (if you are not pregnant) your body produces a hormone that makes this tissue leave the body. This is the body's way of clearing out the womb so it can prepare nice fresh tissue to receive the fertilized egg if a female becomes pregnant. If there is no pregnancy, the body expels the lining of the womb and starts making fresh lining again.

The menstrual cycle repeats itself every month until the menopause when the cycle stops (at about 45-50 years old). The whole cycle is controlled by hormones.

A normal cycle is about 28 days. On day one, the pituitary gland in the brain starts to release two hormones. These travel in the blood stream to the two ovaries in your lower abdomen. The ovaries then start to produce a hormone called estrogen and one ovary prepares an egg for release.

The estrogen hormone affects many other parts of the body as well. In particular, it causes the uterine lining to thicken. It also causes mucus around the cervix (neck-like opening of the uterus) to become more watery. All this takes days.

At about day 14, there is a surge of the two hormones from the brain which cause the ovary to *ovulate* (release its egg). The egg travels through the Fallopian tube to the uterus where it waits. At this time, another hormone called progesterone is released from the ovary to prepare the lining of the womb for the next stage. If the female has sex about this time, a sperm from the male *fertilizes* the egg in the uterus (womb). The egg then nestles into the lining of the womb where it grows and over nine months will develop into a baby.

If the woman hasn't had sex, the egg cannot be fertilized so the ovary stops producing progesterone. The lining of the womb starts to shrink. As it falls away it flows from the womb out through the cervix into the vagina. This bleeding is what you experience as a period every month.

Absorbent sanitary towels and tampons are sold in pharmacies, corner stores, and supermarkets. When they start having periods, most girls start by wearing sanitary towels (inside their pants) to soak up the blood. As they get older and more familiar with the whole process, they usually move on to using tampons which are inserted into the vagina and *must* be changed every 2-3 hours. Your mother or older sister will probably buy your first ones for you and you'll soon get used to carrying some with you whenever you are approaching the time of your period.

If tampons are left in the body too long they can cause toxic shock syndrome which can make you very ill and girls have been known to die of it. So, always change your tampon regularly.

Periods tend to be erratic to begin with but will settle down into a regular pattern after a while. The menstrual cycle varies from one person to another. For some girls, their natural cycle might be over 21 days; for others it might be over 36 days. If you are at all worried about your menstrual cycle, have a chat with your doctor or practice nurse.

Periods can be painful and they affect your whole body in different ways. Many girls find their breasts become very tender just before a period and some tend to get more spots. When you menstruate you may have an awful dull pain in the lower abdomen. A hot water bottle can help, as can simple painkillers. However, if they are persistently very bad you should see your doctor. Don't just suffer in silence!

Premenstrual Tension (PMT): *S*ome women become irritable and depressed a week before their period and may feel bloated, have tender breasts, and have a headache, all of which subsides when the period starts. You may feel as if life is unbearable and you'll never ever be happy again. But don't despair, it will pass and after your period new energy will surge through you. After every period it feels like a fresh start and you feel great again! See also **Anger**.

MOBILE PHONES

There's a lot of concern at the moment that using mobile phones may cause headaches and possibly even cancers of the brain. If you use one get yourself a deflector shield or hands-free headset to use with it. While you don't have one of these protective devices, try to use the phone only briefly or for emergency calls. Having two-hour conversations with your friends on a mobile is not a good idea, and can be expensive too! Carrying a mobile phone, can save you a lot of hassle from your parents if they can call you when they're worried about your safety. Better still, you can call them from anywhere to let them know you'll be late – or if you need help. Many children now prefer to carry a pager.

MOLES (NAEVI)

Moles occur in over 95 percent of white adults. They are defects in the development of the skin caused by pigmented cells clustering together. They may also be hairy. Most white adults have at least 10 moles but are not born with them. They tend to develop later, especially during puberty or pregnancy. They vary in size and appearance, being pink, brown, black, flat or raised, rough or smooth. They have the potential to become a cancer but this is rare. They can easily be removed if they are causing irritation, such as rubbing against a bra strap. See **Cosmetic Surgery**.

It's wise to use a sun-block cream on the moles to reduce the risk of developing skin cancer.

If moles change size, change shape, start to itch or bleed, then you *must* see a doctor as there is a risk they may be turning cancerous.

MORALITY

Having a sense of what is right and wrong is very important in society and is something we all should have. Religious people are given a clear set of guidelines. The rest of us have it passed on to us by our relations and people we come into contact with, or we work it out for ourselves.

Only you can come to the right decision about what you feel to be right or wrong; what is honest and dishonest; what is the responsible way of acting. As you experience life there will be times when you must give serious thought to what is the right thing to do morally. By talking and listening to other people's different points of view then thinking about the issue for yourself, you gradually work out what *you* think is right.

Only you can decide what sort of person you are going to be – nice, horrible, or anything in between! Unfortunately, many people who are really mean and vindictive often seem to get their own way (in the short term) and that makes your decision even more difficult. Do you behave badly, lie, or cheat, to get what you want or do you let it go and move on to something else knowing you've behaved decently? I know what would make me feel best.

MULTIVITAMINS

Multivitamin pills may be necessary to supplement a diet which is deficient in essential minerals and vitamins. But If you eat a sensible balanced diet then you shouldn't need them. See **Food and Nutrition**.

Negative or Positive?

You can choose to take a negative or positive attitude to everything that happens to you. For every high there will be a low. It's natural to feel grim about some things for a while but try not to keep dwelling on the dark side too long. Start looking for a positive way to get the best out of the situation.

NOSEBLEED

If someone gets a nose bleed get them to tip their head forward and pinch the fleshy part of their nose for a few minutes. When the bleeding stops, leave the nose alone and don't let your finger stray into the nostril to dig out the clot!

Nose bleeds are common in teenagers. Inside the nose there's a small area where the blood vessels are very thin and easily damaged by trauma, such as *nose-picking*! There can be more serious causes (blood disorders like hemophilia and high blood pressure) but they are rare. If nosebleeds persist it's wise to see a doctor.

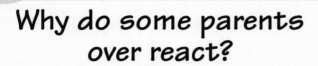

Why *do some parents over react?*

Usually because they're worried about you. You may be out having fun and know you are safe, but if you haven't told them where you are they will worry for hours. When you do finally breeze in, all their fears may suddenly convert into an angry outburst. So phone home!

OPPORTUNITY

Whatever you want to do in life – whether it's to be a neurosurgeon, a mountain climber, a teacher, a trapeze artiste, and/or a mother – my advice is to grasp any opportunities that come along. You may never have another chance to do that particular thing. I often remind myself of something someone once said to me, and I hope you'll think about it too:

**Opportunity only
knocks once.**

Life is not a dress rehearsal!

P

Can you get pregnant standing up?

Yes! So, don't believe all the silly stories and myths that are passed around at school. It's also possible to become pregnant the first time someone has sex. Having a bath immediately after sex will **not** stop pregnancy. The only way to avoid pregnancy is either not have sex or to practice safer sex using a condom!

PARENTS

Love 'em or loathe 'em, one thing is certain, without them you wouldn't be around. Parents come in all varieties, from the young, cool, trendy through the rich, poor, bright, dim, drunken, religious, outdoorsy, big city sophisticates, to the woolly-cardiganed and comfortable. One teenager may have young parents while another has parents as old as another's grandparents. But they are all individuals worthy of your love, interest, trust, and respect; just as you are worthy of theirs.

Being a parent is one of the most rewarding things anyone can ever be but, as in all relationships, parents can go through good and bad patches with their children. Your teenage years could be difficult if you don't try to understand one another's point of view. Life will be easier if you can talk about any issue or conflict calmly and openly, and *listen* to one another. Ask questions like, *What is really worrying you about me doing (or going to) . . .?* Try to reassure them in practical ways if they seem worried. For example, if you say you'll be home at a certain time, make sure you are, or phone to say why you've been delayed. Then maybe next time they'll be happy to extend the deadline.

Radio and TV news items often make the world seem a far scarier place than it mostly is and some parents become very frightened that their teenager may be in danger. If you come home later than expected they will probably have worked themselves into a frenzy of fear for your safety. By the time you get home this fear could be released in an angry outburst that you will feel is completely unjustified. So, do yourselves a favor, work out some ground rules together, and keep to them. If you prove you can be trusted, the rules are more likely to be modified as you get older.

Find a way around problems that will satisfy you all. If you get into a situation where you are fighting one another, neither side will be able to think clearly or inventively enough to find a mutually agreeable solution. If you can modify your behavior a little, you may find them more willing to give you more freedom. Humor usually works better than bad temper to get you what you want.

It may seem your parents are trying to spoil your fun by insisting you are home by eleven or by not allowing you to go to parties on school-week nights. Try to accept that they have your best interests at heart. They know, often from their own experience (!!), that if you party all week you will be too exhausted to concentrate on your schoolwork. They will also know how important getting a good education will be to the choices you will be able to make in the future.

Juliette, 15

One of a family of four children, Juliette was a zany, quick-witted, and popular girl. Her parents were intelligent and caring and had brought up their children to be independent strong characters and trusted all four of them completely. When Juliette asked what time she should be home, her mother would simply say, "It's up to you. Just call if you need us to pick you up or you're staying over with a friend, so we know not to worry. It doesn't matter what time you call, we'd rather be woken up at night than wake and find you not here."

Juliette loved to party and be with her friends but she knew she needed to set herself limits. She wasn't yet ready for such open-ended freedom and would say, "OK, shall I get home by eleven?" And her mother would have to say, "Yes, you must be home by eleven, Jules."

Since Juliette had once been very ill after drinking too much, she didn't like alcohol and could see her friends behaving really stupidly when they got drunk. It bored her and she wanted to be able to leave them to it. And it was easier to get away if she could say, "Bye, my mother says I've got to be home by eleven. See you."

Dr. Dave's Top Tips – Parents

Teenagers can be disgusting creatures. I know was. I used to be very moody, argue all the time, and if I was losing an argument I'd stomp out, slamming all the doors, just to annoy my parents. Which it did but it didn't achieve much else. I suggest you try another tack.

Try a bit of give and take. The bond between you and your parents is vital so try to keep a good relationship with them.

Listen to what your parents say. If you disagree with them, try to explain quietly and logically what you think. Never shout. They will appreciate this.

If you like something they do, tell them.

Make life more fun. Make your parent a fun card occasionally and if you need to leave them a note, try and make it amusing. You'll know their habits; so sticky-tape your note to the first thing they do when they come home – maybe on the toilet seat or the kettle, or over the TV screen, or dangle it from a lampshade in the hall so they walk into it when they come home.

Don't just demand things. Offer something in return, such as, I've done my homework, can I go and play tennis? This is bound to get a better response than, I'm going to play hockey! Stuff the homework!

Try not to squabble constantly with your brothers and sisters.

Telephone if you're going to be late. Don't just rock up when you're good and ready.

Always tell your parents or carer where you're going to be and when you expect to be home.

Agree on some ground rules and keep to them.

Parents often know more than you credit them for. Ask their opinion and for advice. It will please them and may help you to make the right choices for yourself.

Your parents may be just as busy and preoccupied as you are. If you need to talk to them urgently, say so or leave them a note saying you'd like to talk and could you fix a time.

If you only have one parent, you will probably be very reliant on one another. A single parent may be especially protective of you if you are the closest relationship he or she has. They won't want to lose you even though they know you must inevitably develop more and more outside interests as you get older. Your parent may find it hard to see you apparently growing away from them. Reassure them and say you love them but be firm about needing also to be with friends of your own age. If you can get this sorted out early, your gradual move toward independence will be easier and hopefully your parent will begin to appreciate having more time for doing things with their own friends.

Money might be tight in a single-parent family, so try not to get angry and petulant if your parent says he or she can't afford to buy you the latest must-have fashion item. Do something positive. Maybe you can find a Saturday job, baby-sit for neighbors (if you're old enough), offer to wash cars for people you know, have a garage sale and sell your old toys, and save up. You'll feel really proud of yourself the first time you buy your own shoes.

Extra Parents and Step-Parents: As much as we would like our parents to be happy together, sometimes they decide they would be happier with someone else and you end up with two extra adults and maybe other children to get to know and share your life with. It may be difficult for you at first, but try and see it as a bonus. There'll twice as many people to care about you; always somewhere else to stay if things are getting tense in one house; maybe two lots of holidays every year. If you feel angry or jealous about anything, try to talk to your parents calmly about it. If you'd rather speak to someone who's not so involved, try a grandparent, your best friend, an older friend, a teacher, or a child helpline. There's plenty of people who will understand your feelings and talking about them will make it easier for you to see them clearly and work out how to get the best out of the situation.

PEER PRESSURE

It doesn't matter how cool or trendy you are. Whatever you do, whatever you wear, it's always good to feel you're part of a group and that your friends approve of what you do and wear. It's human nature to want to belong and it can be very lonely if you don't find a group of friends who suit you.

Sometimes you may find yourself thinking you have to do something (such as smoking) that you don't really want to, just because everyone else is doing it. That's peer pressure.

Sarah obviously doesn't want to smoke – and it doesn't matter why – it's her decision and if these girls were her true friends they would accept it. If Sarah was being really strong she would stick to her guns and continue to say no. It's possible that the girls would then just accept her for saying no and get on with the party. Or

What should Sarah do?

Sarah is 14. She's very pretty, bright, and quite shy. She and her family recently moved to a new area and Sarah has started at a new school. She found this very difficult and making friends harder still. All this changed when she met a group of girls who she thought were a good laugh. All the girls in the school wanted to belong to their gang. They were it! Cool, funky, wore great clothes, and could have any boy they liked. And they asked Sarah to join their group. This she did and loved it.

Things went well until the party when one of the boys produced some cigarettes. Each girl took a cigarette, lit it, and inhaled deeply. Sarah didn't take one and said she didn't like smoking and it was bad for them. The other girls were outraged. Sarah was told that everyone in the gang smoked and if she wanted to stay in it she should smoke too. And, if she said no then that was it – she would never be part of the girl gang again.

they might chuck her out of the group. At least if the latter happened Sarah would know these girls weren't her real friends after all. But life in the short term would be difficult without her mates and she'd have to start all over again to find new ones.

It's hard to insist on what you believe in against a group of other people. It can seem easier just to go along with them and their ideas. You have to weigh up in your own mind whether it's worth it. In the long run, if you persistently go on being yourself and doing what you want, people will see that you know your own mind and accept and admire you for it.

PERIODS
See **Menstruation.**

PERSONAL HYGIENE
See **Deodorants, Genitals, Fungal Infections.**

PETS
See **Worms:** *Toxocariasis.*

PIMPLES
Pimples are spots. Due to hormonal activity and high intake of refined sugar, pimples erupt on the face of most teenagers. See **Acne.**

PREGNANCY
I really hope no one reading this book has to deal with this issue, but again, it is important to look at what can happen to young girls if they become pregnant.

If a girl thinks she's pregnant because her period is late, she should have a pregnancy test as soon as possible. She should go to a family planning or women's health clinic or her family doctor; or she could buy a pregnancy testing kit from a pharmacist. The test requires a sample of urine and is very easy to do. The kit will give simple instructions. Some pharmacists offer a pregnancy testing service.

If she is pregnant she must get medical advice as soon as possible regardless of whether she wants to keep the baby or talk about other options, such as termination, or possibly having the baby adopted. She shouldn't be put off going to the doctor. The longer she leaves it the fewer options she will have and the more panicky will be her final decision. She is going to have to find a lot of information and do a lot of serious thinking very quickly or before she knows where she is, she will be a mother!

As a teenager, she was probably not planning to get pregnant and will need a great deal of loving support to help her cope with it and help her decide what is best for *her*. If the father is the kind of boy who will help her then she should tell him and talk about all the possibilities and consequences of each option. And if she has the kind of mother or father she can talk to, she should go to them immediately. If not, she should tell any other responsible adult whom she trusts and can ask for help. She can also phone a child helpline for confidential advice. Pretending her pregnancy is not really happening may be OK for a day or two but the sooner she accepts it, the sooner she can start taking responsible action.

If a girl decides to have her baby, it's a good idea to go to libraries and book stores and read everything she can about pregnancy, giving birth, and babies so that she is well prepared. A baby is for life. She is likely to be overwhelmed with love for it and be completely taken over by caring for it for at least the next two years. Gradually, she will find ways of doing the other things that are important to her. If a girl has a baby when she is young and wants to look after it herself, then her education may have to be postponed and she will need to work out how she is going to support herself and her baby. Some girls have a relation who is willing to look after their baby while they are at school.

See also **Blood types**, **Contraception**, **X Chromosomes**, **Termination**.

PUBERTY

Puberty is the time when our body changes from its child shape to being adult. It begins when we are young teenagers and we continue to develop physically until we are about 18.

Are right-handed people brighter than left-handed ones?

No! Whichever hand you use predominantly, you can be just as clever (or dim!) as anyone else.

RAPE

Being forced to have sex against your will (rape) is one of the most violating things that can happen to anyone (it can happen to boys too). It is traumatic at the time but can leave a girl feeling used and dirty, sometimes with a nagging fear that she may have provoked it in some way, which of course isn't true. *No one* has the right to use your body for sex without your permission. Sometimes violence and threats are used and you cannot get away or save yourself. All this can seriously undermine your self-confidence and self-esteem and leave you feeling too nervous to be alone almost anywhere. So the rape not only violates your body it can take away your right to enjoy the rest of your life. This is what you mustn't let happen. You are going to need to talk about what happened and somehow find a way of putting the whole awful business behind you, so that you can live your life fully.

Another awful possibility is that during a rape, life threatening, sexually-transmitted diseases may have been passed on to you. It is essential for anyone who has been raped to report it to the police and to see her doctor as soon as possible.

Wherever you go, whatever you do, you must *always* be aware that rape can happen to anyone.

Never walk alone in the street at night. Avoid dark areas and always let someone know where you are going and when you intend to return.

Carry a rape alarm. They're cheap, easily available, and even if they don't bring anyone to your aid, they may at least frighten off your attacker. Carry the alarm in your hand or in an easily accessible pocket, not buried deep in your handbag! Try to do a self-defense course.

Rapists are not always strangers. They can be people you know and should be able to trust, anyone from a step-father or uncle to an older teenage babysitter. See **Abuse**.

Never leave a window open if it is possible for someone to get through it. Window locks can be fitted to fix it in a slightly opened position if you need to let some air in. And always lock doors at night.

Never get into an unregistered taxi if you're alone nor into an empty railway carriage or bus especially at night. And try always to stay with a group of friends if you come out of a party or club late at night. It's better to stay at your friend's house than to risk walking home, or accepting a lift from a man you've only just met.

Don't Panic! This may be easier said than done. If you can't get away and run as fast as you can to a place of safety, then try to stay calm and try to get a potential rapist to see you as an individual. But he may be mad or on drugs and nothing rational will get through to him.

Do your best to escape from any dangerous situation but always remember that your life is the most important thing for you to protect.

Don't let all this make you too scared to go out. Most boys and men are decent loving individuals who would never harm you. But there are enough rogues about that you must *always* be on your guard.

If you are raped, you will need a lot of love, support, and care. Do find someone to talk to. Call a rape crisis center; they will have trained people who know how to help you.

See also **Alcohol**.

RH NEGATIVE BLOOD
See **Blood Types**.

S

Is salt good for us?

There is no need to add salt to vegetables when they are cooked and you will soon get used to the taste without it. Evidence suggests if you have too much salt in your diet, it increases your blood pressure and that's a bad idea.

SECURITY

Always think of your own safety but don't become so paranoid you stop having any fun. Take simple precautions such as: lock the doors and windows at home, use only licensed taxis, and carry a rape alarm. You're always safer when you're not alone. Don't walk down dark lanes on your own no matter how short the journey. Let someone know where you are and what time you are expected back and call them if you aren't going to make the time.

How should Julie get home?

Julie is 16. She's been dancing in a club until late and needs to get home. It's only a mile up the road and she could easily walk it. What should she do? Her choices are:

1. Get a lift with someone who's been drinking.
2. Get an unregistered taxi that's waiting outside the club.
3. Get a lift with a guy she's just met in the club.
4. Walk.
5. Call her parents.
6. Go home with her friends and call her parents from there to say she's staying the night and that she is safe.

Difficult! But the answer has to be either to call her parents or go with her friends (but not if they're going by car and the driver has been drinking). Although her parents may be grouchy about being woken up, they will be glad that she has acted sensibly and that she is safe.

SEX

Having Sex or Making Love? As you grow up, you'll find many choices opening up to you, all hotly debated in teen magazines! Women want to make love with a man who is very special to them. Even though she has no intention of having a baby yet, instinctively she will be looking for a boy whose genes will produce the best baby, and who would make a good father. Because it is so important to a woman, she is likely to be far more choosy and romantic than a man is about who she first has sex with. She will want it to be with someone she is in love with. Her desire will be to *make love*, whereas a man may just want to *have sex.* Women, because of the knowledge they have of the possible consequences (a baby and 20 years caring for it), may be more selective about their sexual partner than men are.

Having sex too soon may get in the way of falling in love.

As in everything we do, we learn by stages. Nobody ever wanted us to run before we could walk, or sing before we could talk, so in the future, don't be hurried into having sex until you know the time is right for you. If your head and heart are full of romantic expectations, having sex too early may be very disappointing.

It may even mean you miss out on all the pleasures of getting to know one another properly and really falling in love with someone you have come to care deeply about.

Until we know how to have fun together, to be friends, to work and play together, to really know and care for one another as individuals, we are not going to get the best out of the intimate act of having sex. We need time to discover ourselves and one another and our bodies, with spaces in between each encounter to assimilate what is happening, to think clearly about it, consider consequences, and to decide for ourselves what we want to do.

**The right time, place, and person,
is different for everyone.**

Young women whose first sexual experience is not as special as they had imagined may regret that they didn't give themselves more time to indulge in their romantic dreams and longings, and to build up a good relationship. Young women may think making love is going to be a beautiful act but until both participants are mature enough to make it so, it may not be. In fact, the first few times are often awkward and clumsy.

Don't forget that for very good reasons in most countries it is illegal for a man to have sex with a girl under 16.

See **Abuse, AIDS, Contraception, HIV, Pregnancy, Termination of Pregnancy, Sexually Transmitted Infections**.

A recent survey in the U.S.A. revealed that *over 80 percent* of the young women interviewed regretted the first time they had sex and *over 90 percent* of them wished they had waited until they were older!

SEXUALLY TRANSMITTED INFECTIONS (STI)

If anyone has unprotected sex (without using a condom), they run the risk of contracting a sexually transmitted infection or disease. STI are all very unpleasant and some can cause fertility problems which may make it difficult to conceive a baby in the future. AIDS will cause death.

Gonorrhea causes vaginal discharge, pain on passing urine, and bleeding between periods. It's the commonest cause of acquired infertility. It can be treated with antibiotics.

Chlamydia causes belly pain and fever. It can also cause infertility. It can be treated with antibiotics.

Syphilis starts with a spot which grows to form a painless ulcer and causes the glands in the groin to swell up. Four weeks later the person begins to feel ill with a fever, sore throat and a rash develops. Other glands start to swell up and lots of ulcers start to appear in the mouth and on the genitals. If it is not treated, it goes on to affect the skin and the bones, the heart, and the nervous system and that can lead to meningitis, problems walking, and dementia. It can be treated with antibiotics.

Herpes causes multiple painful ulcers on the genitals; groin glands to swell up; and a fever and headache. The ulcers dry up and heal. But once an individual is infected with this virus, it remains with them forever and they can have repeat attacks at any time, especially when they are run down. Antiviral treatments are helpful. See also **Cold Sores**.

Warts are caused by a virus. They are fleshy growths on the genitals. There is an increased risk of cervical cancer with some types.

Thrush, a severe vaginal itch and a white discharge. See **Candida Albicans.**

Lice: Itchiness around the genital area. See **Lice**.

HIV and AIDS: There is a very real risk that women or men can contract HIV from unprotected sex. It is not just a gay disease; heterosexual people get it too. The HIV virus leads to AIDS which leads to death. See **AIDS** and **HIV**.

SLEEP

We spend a third of our lives asleep. If we don't get enough sleep, next day we are irritable and our performance is sluggish. Anyone permanently unable to sleep would die.

Sleeping is a time of great activity! While we sleep our cells continue to function as our body repairs itself. Our brain is very active, sorting out what we have experienced during the day, storing important information as memory and discarding anything irrelevant. Also, our sub-conscious mind works away at our

Dr. Dave's Top Tips to Sleep Easy

Unwind before going to bed. At least an hour before bedtime, stop working, talking on the phone, dancing, or any other form of exercise. Your brain needs time to slow down.

Avoid any stimulants in the evening such as cigarettes, tea, coffee, cola, chocolate. A milky drink may help.

Do some exercise during the day.

Drink 6-8 glasses of plain water throughout the day so you are not dehydrated.

Take a hot bath with a few drops of relaxing essential oil of lavender in it.

Keep your bedroom cool. It's impossible to sleep if you're too hot.

Try not to toss and turn, it reminds your brain that you're still awake. Try not to get angry or upset about *not* sleeping; sleep won't come until you're relaxed.

ZZZZZzzzzzzzzzzzzzzzzzzzzzzzzzzzzzzzzzz

problems overnight. That's why we often wake up knowing what we have to do, or with a great idea, or some great plan.

As well as all that, teenagers are *growing* their adult bodies while they sleep, which is why they need 8–10 hours a night.

There are different stages of sleep. Within the first 20 minutes of falling asleep we enter the first phase known as *deep sleep*. During this period, sleep deepens and various hormones are released including growth hormone.

The second phase of sleep is known as REM (rapid eye

movement). During REM most of the body's muscles are paralyzed, apart from the heart and the muscles controlling the eyes and the diaphragm. We dream in this second phase and the dreams can be very scary or energetic. We often dream of running, walking, or flying, and if our muscles were not in a state of paralysis then we might harm ourselves.

Scientific research is still being done to find out more about sleep. But we do know that sleep is vital if we are to stay fit and healthy. However, excitement, tension, fear, or worrying can cause sleep disturbances such as teeth grinding, sleepwalking and, most commonly, insomnia which means being unable to get off to sleep.

SMOKING

Kissing a smoker tastes foul. Yeugh! Smoking robs your skin of its youthful freshness and in no time at all you'll be looking like an old hag. All your clothes and hair will reek. So will those of your non-smoking friends and they'll hate it. Besides which, smoking is addictive and expensive. You'll soon be a slave to nicotine and to the happy manufacturers who want to stay filthy rich at your expense.

Some of the Toxic Chemicals in Tobacco Smoke	
4-Aminobiphenyl	Causes bladder cancer.
Carbon Monoxide	Lowers oxygen levels.
Hydrogen Cyanide	Lung irritant.
Tar	Possible source of carcinogens (cancer causing chemicals).
Nicotine	Causes addiction.
Nitrosamines	The most active cancer-causing agent in tobacco.
Polycyclic aromatic hydrocarbons	Carcinogenic (cancer causing).

Why is it, when so many people have grasped the scientific evidence about the dangers of smoking and given up, the only group who are smoking more are teenage girls? Your friends may try to convince you that it's cool to smoke but it's not, it's *stupid*. It seriously damages your health. If you smoke, some of the horrors you may be storing up for your future are:

Breathing Problems: Smoking makes asthma worse. It causes long-term damage and causes bronchitis and emphysema. At the moment, you don't even think about breathing, but can you imagine finding it difficult to walk across a room because you can only just about gasp in enough breath to keep you alive? That's what it's like to have emphysema.

Heart Disease: Half the people you know will die of a heart attack. Smoking is a major cause of heart problems.

Pregnancy Problems: Every cell of a developing fetus needs oxygen. Smoking reduces the amount of oxygen getting to your baby, making it more likely to be born undersized. It causes babies to be born prematurely and increases the chance of miscarriage. You might say, "Oh, well, I'd give up smoking if I got pregnant," but by then you will be well and truly hooked and giving up may be a lot harder than you can imagine.

Cancer: Smoking directly causes cancer of the lungs, esophagus (food pipe), and mouth. Smoking 20 cigarettes a day makes you four times more likely to get breast cancer.

How not to start smoking

1. You will probably want to try it for yourself, so have a puff the first time you're offered one, then cough and splutter and swear loudly that you're *never ever* going to smoke. It won't be hard; breathing in hot cigarette smoke is horrible.
2. Invent and try out at home all the ways you can think of to say no to a proffered cigarette. If you can't bring yourself just to

say, *No thanks, it's bad for me, it's disgusting*, or, *I hate the smell*, try some white lies. They're justifiable in this case and your parents won't mind if you pretend it's them who are restricting you. Here are some suggestions but I bet you can come up with even better ones. (Write and tell me them, c/o the publisher of this book, so I can pass them on to other kids. *Dr. Dave.*)

- *No thanks, I don't smoke.*
- *No thanks, smoke brings me out in a rash.*
- *No thanks, if I come home smelling of smoke I'll be grounded for month.*
- *No thanks, those cigarette companies ain't getting their greedy hands on my money.*

3. Always have your hands full, with a bag, some magazines, a can of drink, a computer game, etc.

Stop!

Copy this advice and give it to a smoker

1. Make the decision to stop smoking – NOW.

2. Get a friend or relative to give up at the same time. The mutual sympathy *and* the competition will help you both.

3. Get rid of any cigarettes, lighters, ashtrays, anything that will remind you of your old habit.

4. Never buy cigarettes or look after anyone else's.

5. Refuse if anyone offers you a cigarette, saying firmly, *No thanks, I don't smoke.*

6. Save the money you would have spent on cigarettes and give yourself little rewards. At first it might be just a glossy magazine, some new make-up, or something else you've had to go without so you could buy cigarettes. After a month, you'll probably have saved enough to buy some CDs. In a year, who knows?

7. Find things to do which don't involve people smoking. Smoking is not allowed in most cinemas or public buildings today. Go swimming, join a sports club, learn a relaxation technique such as Tai Chi or Yoga. Put on a CD in your bedroom and dance. When you can breathe properly you'll be able to dance all night instead of gasping for air after five minutes.

8. If you hang out with smokers, always take a can or bottle of something to drink with you so that you, too, have something to move from hand to mouth.

See also **Willpower**.

SNORING

Sleeping in the same room with a snorer would ruin anyone's beauty sleep.

Snoring occurs when the soft palate at the top back of the mouth relaxes so much that it vibrates as you breathe. You are more likely to snore if you are overweight, you smoke, or when you have a cold, hay fever, or any other condition that causes inflammation of the throat. Sleeping on your back makes it worse.

SPIRIT

We sense in ourselves and in other people an awareness that has no physical substance. We can't touch it or see it, or adequately describe it, yet this vital life force is the very essence of our being. It is sometimes called our soul, or spirit. It is the source of who we are; it is at the heart of our instincts and understanding; it is the safe place from which we venture into the world and to which we may retreat at any time; it is our inner strength. And it is inexhaustible. It will be with you all your life. No matter what you put your body through, your spirit will be there, safe and strong, humming along quietly, supporting *you* – no questions asked.

SPORTS

Have a go at all the sports that are on offer until you find the ones you enjoy. If you really dislike one, don't let anyone bully you into doing it. Suggest to your teacher or parents that you try something else. Doing sports is a great way to keep fit, take in some fresh air, get to know yourself, make friends, and discover how to work together in a team. Keeping in shape and excelling in sports does wonders for your self-esteem and confidence and you'll love the admiration you get. And exercise that gets your heart working hard at least three times a week is good for it and you. As you work at your sport you'll be learning how to focus your mind as well as coordinate your body effectively. See *Mind Games* in **Further Reading.**

Pressure to Perform: If you have a special talent for a particular sport, you will probably start off really enjoying it. Then you may find trainers and parents are pressurizing you to spend every minute training or preparing for it. Talk to them about it, try to explain how you're feeling and that you need to have a better balance in you life, that you need to see friends and be part of what's going on.

Embarrassing Moments: Communal changing rooms can be embarrassing for some young girls and spoil all the fun of a sport they really like. You may be feeling shy about your body, the way it's changing, breasts growing or *not* growing, the hairy bits... It's no good pretending no one will look at you (they will) but they'll be looking at *everyone* not just at you. Also, most of them will be just as worried as you are about everyone looking at them. If it's a serious problem for you, make sure you take the biggest towel you can find and dress under it. If you really, really can't bear it, talk to your mother or some older female you can trust and see if you can work out a better solution than hooking off school on sports day. Most grown-ups will remember how it was for them and be sympathetic.

See also **Water**.

SPOTS

See **Acne**.

STRESS

When you say you are feeling "stressed out" it usually means you are under pressure at home, school, your sports club, or a combination of all kinds of things that are making you feel tense, worried, or fearful. These are normal pressures and your body and mind are well equipped to cope with them. This is not stress.

The word *stress* is often wrongly used to describe normal pressures in our lives without which many of us wouldn't get out of bed in the morning, make it to the bus stop in time, or pass any exams. Such pressure is an extension of what drove our ancestor's out to hunt and gather their daily food. So, as a species we have had plenty of practice in dealing with it. Some pressure is good for us. It causes our body to release stimulating chemicals, such as adrenaline, which help us to perform better.

Stress is a chemical reaction that occurs when you need an extra boost, perhaps to accelerate your reactions to avoid a speeding car, to get you through an exam, or to give you the courage to speak to a gorgeous guy. But when you're under a lot of pressure for a long time, your brain, heart, lungs, and muscles are constantly being stimulated by extra adrenaline and other stress chemicals. If it goes on too long you become exhausted and are liable to get sick – perhaps your body's way of saying "take a break."

Dr. Dave's Top Tips – Coping with Stress

Exercise burns up stress chemicals but over-exercising or over-tiredness, cause stress.

Your heart will thump away to get you through a first date or a big test, but when you get home, I bet you flop down exhausted on your bed. Quite natural. A good meal and a night's rest and you'll be raring to do it all over again.

If you find yourself living in constant fear of someone or some situation, find a responsible caring adult to talk to. If there's no one you can trust, try calling some of the organizations listed at the back of this book that are relevant to your problem. Your school, local libraries, and telephone directories will have similar lists. Keep going until you get the help you need.

Relaxation techniques produce anti-stress chemicals in your body. If you can't afford to take a course, get a book out of the library and teach yourself. Perhaps do it with a group of friends so you can encourage each other to do it regularly.

SUNTAN AND PROTECTION

Of course, girls look startlingly beautiful with a suntan. But is there a safe way of getting one? How safe are sunbeds?

We need sunlight to stay healthy. It improves our mood and it helps our body to produce vitamin D but too much of the sun's rays can be dangerous. They are made up of light that we can see and some we can't. The light we can't see is called ultraviolet or UV light. Most is deflected by the ozone layer between the Earth

---

Dr. Dave's Top Tips – Tanning

Prevention is always better than cure, so:

Always use suncream: You really should use factor 15 or higher at all times and check that there are four stars on the bottle. This means it will protect you against UVA light. The factor number means it will protect you for 15 times longer against UVB light. Re-apply it frequently and don't forget the bits of you that stick out, such as your nose and ears.

Wear a hat and sunglasses and make sure the sunglasses comply to safety standards.

Avoid the midday sun when it is at its hottest.

You can burn even on cloudy days.

Look out for any changes to moles or freckles. You should see a doctor if a mole or freckle has increased in size, if it itches, bleeds, or changes color.

If you do get burned put lots of soothing cream on the burn; aloe vera will help. Calamine lotion will also help. Drink lots of fluids (especially water). Seek medical help.

---

and the sun but as this has become thinner more harmful rays are reaching the Earth's surface. When the skin is exposed to this UV light, a chemical called melanin is produced in the skin and turns it brown. This is part of the body's attempt to protect itself.

Too much sun causes our skin to age, it can burn you and can lead to skin cancer. Even in the UK over 40,000 people are diagnosed with skin cancer each year and it's even worse in hot countries such as America and Australia. We also know that the biggest risk for getting skin cancer is being burned when you are under 15 years of age.

Sun-beds are not very safe. It used to be thought they were a safer way to tan because they only used UVA light *but* we now know that this ages the skin and may still lead to cancers. It is not recommended to use sun-beds.

Safe color: There is an increasing array of products that can be used to give you a tan. Fake tans have improved and no longer make you as orange as a carrot! There's no evidence of harmful effects apart from a dermatitis which people with sensitive skin may suffer from.

Bag it and Bin it!

Tampons, their applicators, and sanitary towels should be disposed of in a waste bin rather than flushed down toilets. Flushed down the toilet they can cause blockages in the plumbing and block filters in central processing plants.

TAMPONS OR SANITARY TOWELS?
See **Menstruation**.

TATTOOS
See **Body Art.**

TEMPERATURE
Any temperature above 37.5°C is a sure sign that your body is fighting an infection. If it persists and is accompanied by other symptoms, you should see a doctor. See also **Fever,** and **Meningitis**.

TERMINATION OF PREGNANCY (TOP)
Sometime in your life, you or someone you know may have to consider making a very difficult decision.

In an ideal world *all* pregnancies would be wanted and every baby treasured. Sadly, this is not the case. If a woman becomes pregnant and the child is not wanted then it is medically possible to terminate the pregnancy. It can be done in several ways but the methods used vary according to the law in each country. Ask your doctor, teacher, or health adviser what the law is where you live. Specialist organizations exist to advise and help pregnant women. Be aware, though, that some are morally against abortion (which they see as killing an unborn child) no matter what the circumstances are for an individual woman; while others will give her all the practical advice, information, and support she needs so that she can make her own informed decision. She should speak to them all because it will help her to consider all points of view before making her own balanced decision about what is right for *her* in her circumstances.

A normal pregnancy lasts for 40 weeks. In England and Wales it is legal for a termination to be carried out within the first 24 weeks

Sarah's Dilemma

Sarah came to see me when I was working as a general practitioner in London. She was 14, bright, and looking forward to going to University but her life came to a crushing halt when she realized she was pregnant. She felt she couldn't tell her mother and she didn't know what to do. For Sarah, having the baby would have been disastrous. She would have had to drop out of school early. She would have missed her chance to go to university. She would see her friends being free to go out and have fun while she had to look after her baby 24 hours a day for most of the first year. She knew all this and so did I.

The most important thing I did was to get her to talk about it with her mother. It took me two weeks but it worked. At first her mother was shocked but her concern and love for her daughter prevailed and it brought them closer together. They were able to discuss and consider all the possible options and Sarah decided that she had to have a termination. Luckily, the pregnancy was in its very early stages and a termination was arranged.

I saw Sarah some years later. She had passed her final year exams and now has a university place to study law. She does not regret her decision.

(six months) only *if* the mother or baby's life or physical or mental health is in danger. It is felt to be wrong to terminate a pregnancy after this because the baby will be sufficiently developed at 24 weeks to survive outside the mother's body.

**Termination (abortion) is *not*
a substitute for contraception.**

The best way for a woman to ensure she doesn't need a termination is to make sure all pregnancies are planned. That means using proper contraception whenever she has sex.

Although I agree with the groups who believe abortion is taking the life of an unborn child and should be avoided if possible, I don't think it's always as black and white as that. Termination is not an easy option but there are some circumstances where it may be the best option.

See also **Pregnancy**; **Sex**; **Sexually Transmitted Diseases**; **Rape**; and **Support Groups**.

THRUSH

Thrush is an infection that affects moist areas of the body such as the vagina and, less often, the anus and mouth. It is caused by *candida albicans*, a yeast that is naturally present in everyone's body. The yeast multiplies when the normal bacterial balance in the body has been disturbed, perhaps after a course of antibiotics (which kill off good as well as bad bacteria). Oral contraceptives and antibiotics both alter the normal bacterial content of the body and can provide conditions in which candida can thrive.

Candida is also likely to multiply if you exhaust yourself working and playing for too long without regularly eating and sleeping well; and if you wear tight-fitting synthetic pants or tights that create the warm, moist conditions so right for candida to grow in.

Symptoms are: Itchiness, soreness, and redness of the vagina; abnormal white vaginal discharge that has a yeasty smell. After puberty some vaginal discharge is normal, especially in the two weeks before you menstruate.

See **Candida Albicans**, and **Genitals**.

TRUST

Trust is immensely important in relationships. Knowing who you can trust and likewise being trustworthy yourself will ensure lasting friendships even after a relationship breaks up. If someone trusts you enough to tell you their darkest secret, keep it. If you think they need help, talk to them about what to do, get their agreement before going to a responsible adult for help if necessary. Reassure them that you will be available to them if they need support in whatever they should do.

URINARY TRACT INFECTION (UTI)

These are common and are caused by bacteria which crawl up the urethra (the pipe from the bladder to the outside of the body through which urine is passed) to the bladder where they multiply.

Symptoms are pain in the lower abdomen, and needing to go to the toilet more often than usual, and there's a burning pain when you pass urine.

Urinary tract infections can be very serious because the bacteria can crawl up the ureter from the bladder to reach the kidneys and an infection of the kidneys is very painful. It can scar the kidney and stop it working. It's important to treat the infection early with antibiotics from the doctor.

Dr. Dave's Top Tips to prevent UTI

Drink lots of water: 6-8 glasses a day.

Always wipe yourself from front to back after going to the toilet.

Vegetables and Fruit

These are great for keeping your body working well. Eat some every day — the fresher the better.

VACCINATION
See **Immunization** and **Further Reading**.

VAGINA
This is the moist canal that has an opening between your legs. It leads up to the womb and is sometimes called the birth canal

because a baby is both conceived and leaves its mother's body through it.

See **Genitals**, and **Sex**.

VEGANS AND VEGETARIANS
See **Food and Nutrition**.

VENEREAL DISEASE (VD)
See **Sex,** and **Sexually Transmitted Infections**.

VERRUCA (PLANTAR WART)
See **Warts and Verrucas**.

WARTS AND VERRUCAS
A wart is a scaly overgrowth of skin which is set off by a viral infection. Common warts grow on the hands and without treatment usually go away within 3-6 months, but sometimes take a year or two. Warts are highly infectious; you catch them from other people.

Verrucas (plantar warts) are warts that grow in the sole of your foot. You catch them by direct contact with the *papilloma virus.* The virus lurks in damp places such as swimming pool changing rooms, bathrooms, and showers after someone with a verruca has been there without covering it. To protect you or to stop you spreading verrucas to other people, plastic socks are available at many pools.

A verruca starts as a tiny pink area with black specks (tiny blood clots) and may become dark brown with a rough surface. It does you no harm but is best treated to avoid spreading them to other people.

Dr. Dave's Top Tips – Warts and Verrucas

Eat lots of green and orange vegetables to increase your intake of Vitamin A and zinc.

If you can't face waiting for warts to go away naturally, buy a pumice stone and a wart or verruca treatment from the pharmacist or drugstore.

First, pare down the wart with the pumice stone.

Follow instructions exactly and apply the wart ointment or gel to the affected area only so you don't burn the surrounding skin.

Persist with the treatment every day, even when you get really bored with it or are pushed for time.

Large verrucas can be treated by a doctor. He or she will either freeze them off with liquid nitrogen, or cut or scrape them off surgically.

WATER

Every cell in our body needs water. It makes up sixty percent of our body weight. Without water we could not live. The balance of water is minutely monitored by your body as it constantly uses and loses water through your breath, perspiration, stools, and urine. If you lose more than you take in, you feel thirsty and your kidneys compensate by drawing water from your blood which makes your urine dark yellow. Any excess water in the body is peed out as clear-colored urine.

Dr. Dave's Top Tips – Water

Avoid becoming dehydrated. Drink at least 6-8 glasses of water during every day. And more in hot weather or if you do a lot of physical exercise.

Don't confuse other fluids with water. Drinks that contain caffeine (tea, coffee, fizzy drinks), alcohol, or sugars (even the natural ones found in fruit juice) cause dehydration. Follow every such drink with a glass of water.

If dehydrated, slowly replenish water by sipping some with a little salt or sugar alternately added to each glass. If in a sporting situation, you may be offered a specially prepared electrolyte solution in water to replace lost body salts and glucose.

Drink water at room temperature. Believe it or not, your body prefers it to iced water.

Dehydration – Acute

Young adults who exercise or play fast sports which cause them to sweat a lot, especially in hot or humid conditions, can suffer from dehydration.

Symptoms include muscle cramps, thirst (dry lips and mouth), tiredness, muscle fatigue, and dry skin (no sweat). If dehydration becomes *severe*, dizziness or fainting, rapid heartbeat, and mental confusion may occur.

Dehydration – Chronic

Chronic (persistent) dehydration occurs when your body adjusts to never getting sufficient water. Unless they get enough water, our cells rebel. They seal in the water they do have, which prevents the essential free flow of water in and out of them. This prevents the efficient elimination of toxins from the body which can cause a variety of illnesses, and weight gain.

Health Benefits of Water

Skin: Water keeps your skin looking fresh and healthy by supporting proteins such as collagen and elastin.

Boil the Bugs

Even water treated to very high standards will still have some bugs in it when it comes out of the tap. Healthy bodies get used to destroying these bugs, so they don't usually make us sick. However, anyone whose immune system has been working hard to fight off an infection or which isn't working properly, should always boil tap water before drinking it.

Bowels: Drinking water helps your bowel to function properly. It reduces the risk of constipation (especially if you eat plenty of fiber) and the risk of irritable bowel syndrome.

Other structures: Water aids the recovery of damaged muscles and tendons, and keeps the lining of many parts of the body healthy.

Soft and fruit drinks can contain up to five teaspoons of sugar so they aren't exactly good for you!

WILLPOWER

You may *want* to switch off the TV and do your homework, or to give up eating candy; to stop biting your fingernails; or to play the guitar well, but unless you tune up your will*power* it'll never happen. Here's how to do it:

Make a decision. Decide what you want to do (or not do) and when you're going to start (as soon as possible and don't postpone it). Say out loud what you intend to do and/or write it down.

Maybe make a deal with someone you care about. You might agree with your brother, mother, or father, that if they give up smoking, you'll stop biting your nails.

Think of a reward to give yourself at the end of the first week, then two weeks later, then three weeks after that.

Keep a diary or stick up a list of numbers 1-30 in a room you both use (perhaps next to the bathroom mirror). Beside the numbers make a column for you and whoever else is battling for self-control. Each evening, each of you put a check or a cross in your own column depending on whether or not you have succeeded or failed in your aim that day.

Distract yourself. Get through the first hour by going out or doing something that really occupies your brain and hands. Similarly get through the next hour, then the next. Celebrate with lots of self-congratulation when you've successfully got through half a day, and again at the end of the day. Bit by bit it *will* get easier.

If you're a nail biter it may help to begin with if you wear gloves at the times when you usually nibble your nails. Find a way to jolt yourself into noticing when you're about to do whatever it is that has become a habit. Say to yourself, "No, I'm not going to do . . ."

If you want to do your music practice or your homework early, set a loud alarm clock for a convenient time. Place it out of reach where it will be impossible to ignore when it goes off so you'll have to get up to switch it off. When it rings, force yourself to go and do your work immediately. Don't think about doing it, go and *do it.*

Once you've proved you can control what you want to do by using your own willpower, there's no end to what you'll be able to achieve. It feels good to know what you want to do, to take control, and to know you've succeeded in doing it.

WIND

It is natural and healthy to fart 10-20 times a day. However, it's *not* considered "good manners" to do it in public, especially in an enclosed space. It is thought that holding in the gas may be one of the causes of irritable bowel syndrome. So, when you feel the need, take a walk outside or go to the toilet and let rip.

WORMS

Fortunately, worms are not a huge problem in non-tropical countries but the very thought of them living in your gut is enough reason to know how to recognize and get rid of them.

Roundworms (nematodes) and threadworms (pinworms): These thin white worms are the most common and can grow up to half an inch (1 cm) long. They cause no symptoms while in your gut, but at night the female lays its eggs which cause itchiness around your rectum (anus). Don't scratch and get them under your fingernails; you won't want worms for breakfast will you? They won't do you any serious harm but you should get them treated.

Toxocariasis: This is a condition caught from the worms that infest cats and dogs. You may get them on your hands as you stroke your pets or from the grass where they have defecated, then transfer them to the food you eat. The worms don't develop in humans but their larvae can enter vital organs via the bloodstream and cause obstruction of blood vessels when they die. Make sure your pets are regularly wormed (given worming pills). Wash your hands after handling pets and always before you eat. And, nice as it is, kissing pets is not a good idea!

Tapeworms (cestodes): These parasites can grow up to 26 feet (8 m) long in three months. You may not have any symptoms but if you unexpectedly start losing weight, don't feel like eating, and have vague stomach pains, check your poo for segments of tape-like worm.

Dr. Dave Recommends

If you think you may have worms see your doctor who will prescribe a drug to get rid of them. Your whole family and possibly your classmates may have to be treated at the same time to prevent re-infestation.

X-RAYS

An X-ray machine is a wonderful invention and a great aid to doctors when they need to see what's going on inside you, perhaps how and where a bone is broken. They can then decide on the best treatment. Low dosage dental X-rays can help a dentist see if the roots of your teeth are in a twist or are infected.

An X-ray passes ionizing radiation through the body to make a picture on film. A healthy body can deal with the small amount of radiation when a single X-ray is done. But too many, done too close together, may harm body cells and predispose them to cancer. So:

Keep very still while having an X-ray. This will avoid having to have another X-ray done because movement blurred the first one.

Initially, X-rays may be necessary but never be afraid to tell a radiologist if you have already had a lot done. Suggest that you may not need an X-ray at the final check-up if your limb can be checked just as well by feeling the injured part and asking *you* how it is. After all, you will know better than anyone whether or not your limb is back in good working order.

Modern X-ray machines direct the rays very accurately but still insist on having the rest of your body, especially breasts and ovaries, protected by a lead apron. Radiation can damage the eggs in your ovaries and perhaps harm the babies you may want to have years after breaking a leg!

X CHROMOSOMES

A fetus becomes male or female depending on whether it inherits X or Y chromosomes from its father.

Girls' cells have two X chromosomes (XX). Boys' cells have one X and one Y chromosome (XY). When a male and a female mate and have a baby, chromosomes from each of them are passed on to it. The female only has X chromosomes to donate but the male can provide *either* X or Y. If the resulting combination is XY the baby will be a boy, and if it's XX it will be a girl!

The chances of having a boy or a girl are 50:50.

Chromosomes are made of DNA which is the material that carries the characteristics you inherit from your parents. Each baby from the same parents inherits a different set of the parents' genes, which is why brothers and sisters look similar but different to one another.

YOU

You are *unique*. There is only one of you and everything about *you* makes you special. The very particular mix of what you have inherited from your parents and what you experience in life is yours alone. It is what makes you of special interest. It's what you have to center your life on.

So, don't waste your precious time trying to be something utterly impossible. Make the most of what *you* are. That may even include making the "impossible" possible!

We all want perfect teeth, better brains, to look gorgeous, hold an audience spellbound with our brilliant wit, be rich, successful, thin – you name it, someone wants it. And you can guarantee anyone who has all those things will still be wanting to be more like someone else.

All our lives we make choices from which we learn and develop who we are. Your teen years are a time to experiment, to discover what *you* do and don't like, how you want to be, and how you want other people to see you. It's a big world with lots of exciting and sometimes troubling choices to sift through. We all make some mistakes but there's always tomorrow to choose another direction based on what you've learned about yourself and other people. It can take years to discover who *you* are and what *you* really want out of life.

Talk and listen to other people but try always to know and do what *feels right for you.*

GET TO KNOW YOURSELF.

BE STRONG INSIDE.

BE **YOU**.

Z

ZZZZZZZZZZZZZZZZZZZZZZZZZ

Teenagers need at least 8 and often 10 hours
sleep a night. You have a lot of growing to do and
it only happens while you're asleep. So, snuggle
down, close your eyes — you need no further
excusezzzzzzzzzzzzzzzzzzzzzzzzzzzzzzzzzzzzzz z z z

z
z
z

ZITS

Zits, spots, pimples, whatever you call them there's not many lucky
teenagers who don't have them. See **Acne** for how to live with
them.

SUPPORT GROUPS AND HELPLINES

No matter what you need, there is usually an organization with sympathetic people you can talk to. They will give you confidential help, information, and advice, or tell you where else to look for it. The following addresses and phone numbers will get you started in your search but your local phone directory will contain more comprehensive lists specific to your area.

ACNE

UK **Acne Support Group**
PO Box 230, Hayes, Middlesex, UB4 OUT.
Telephone: 0181 561 6868

USA **American Academy of Dermatology**
930 N. Meachum Road, P.O. Box 4014,
Scaumburg, IL 60168.
Internet: http://www.aad.org/

AIDS HELPLINES

UK **National AIDS Helpline**
Freephone: 0800-567123

USA **Center** for Disease Control
National AIDS Hotline
Telephone: 1800-342-2437

ALCOHOL

UK **Alcoholics Anonymous**
Telephone: 0345 697555 or 01904 644026/7/8/9.

Al-Anon Family Groups
Help for the family of anyone who has a drinking problem. They will put you in touch with your nearest **Alateen** *self-help group.*
Telephone: 0171 403 0888.

USA   **Al-Anon Family Group Headquarters, Inc.**
1600 Corporate Landing Parkway,
Virginia Beach, VA 23454.
Internet: http://www.Al-Anon-Alateen.org/
Telephone: (757) 563-1600.

ALLERGIES
UK   **The British Allergy Foundation**
30 Bellegrove Road, Welling, Kent, DA16 3PY.
Telephone: 0181-3038525

USA   **Asthma** and Allergy Foundation of America (AAFA)
1233 20th ST, NW, Suite 402,
Washington, DC 20038
Internet: http://www.aafa.org/
Telephone: (202) 466-7643.

CANCER
UK   **Macmillan Cancer Relief**
Telephone: 0171-3517811
For counselling phone: 0171-8232451.

USA   **Cancer Communications**
Bldg. 31, Rm. 10A16, BETHESDA, MD 20892.
Telephone: 1800-422-6273.

American Cancer Society
1599 Clifton Road, NE, Atlanta, GA 30329-4251.
Telephone: (212) 320-333.

CHILDREN AS CARERS

UK   **Carersline**
*For advice call Monday-Friday
between* 10 a.m. to 12 p.m. or 2-4 p.m.
Freephone: 0808-808-7777.

USA   **National Family Caregivers Association**
9621 E. Beckshill Drive, Kensington, MD 20895.
Telephone: (301) 942-6430.

COLD SORES

UK   **Herpes Viruses Association**
41 North Road, London, N7 9DP.
Helpline: 0171-6099061.

COSMETIC SURGERY – FIND AN EXPERT

UK   *Write enclosing a stamped, self-addressed, envelope
(sae) to any of these organizations requesting a list of
accredited members who have met stringent standards
of practice.*

**British Association of Aesthetic Plastic Surgeons of
England (BAAPS)**
The Royal College of Surgeons
35-43 Lincoln's Inn Fields London WC2A 3PN.
(Send *large* sae.)
Telephone: 0171-4052234.

British Association of Dermatologists (BAD),
BAD House, 19 Fitzroy Square, London W1P 5HQ.
Telephone: 0171-3830266.

General Medical Council (GMC)
*Helpline to confirm whether a doctor or plastic surgeon
has completed a recognized course of specialist training.*
Telephone: 0171-9153630.

Institute of Electrolysis
138 Downs Barn Blvd, Milton Keynes, MK14 7RP.
Telephone: 01908-695297.

BREAST CARE

UK   **Breast Care Campaign**
http://www.breastcare.co.uk
*Dispels myths and addresses common fears. Also has a
useful monthly breast pain monitoring chart.*

DOMESTIC VIOLENCE

UK   **Women's Aid National Helpline**
Telephone: 0345 023468 (local rates)

USA   **National Domestic Violence Hotlines**
Telephone tollfree: 1800-799-72233 or 1800-6218HOPE

DRUGS

UK   **Release Emergency Service** (24-hour)
Telephone: 0171 603 8654.

       Turning Point
Telephone: 0171-702 2300.

USA   **National Council on Alcoholism & Drug Dependence**
Telephone tollfree: 800-622-2255 or 800-475-4673.

EMERGENCY SERVICES

For police, ambulance, fire, coastguard, mountain or cave rescue, phone:

UK   Telephone: 999.
USA   Telephone: 911.

DRY SKIN & ECZEMA

UK   **National Eczema Society**
163 Eversholt Street, London, NW1 1BU
Telephone: 0171 388 4097.

HEADACHE & MIGRAINE

UK   **British Migraine Association**
178A High Road, Byfleet, Surrey KT14 7ED.
Telephone: 01932 352468.

Migraine Trust
45 Great Ormond Stree, London WC1N 3HZ.
Telephone: 0171 831 4818.
(Ask for support services.)

HEALTH AND SAFETY

UK   **Health and Safety Executive**
Gas Safety Advice Line
Freephone: 0800 300 363.

HEALTH INFORMATION

UK   **National Health Service (NHS)**
For services and treatment, including details of self-help groups, lists of doctors and dentists, information on local hospitals and details of how to make a complaint.
Freephone: 0800-665544.

USA **Kid's Health at AMA**
American Medical Association
515 North State Street, Chicago, IL 60610.
Telephone: (312) 464-5000.

Dept. of Health and Human Services
Internet: http://health.org/gpower
Telephone: (202) 619-0257.

HELPLINES

UK **ChildLine**
Freepost 1111, London N1 OBR
Help and support for any young person in trouble.
Free*fone*: 0800 1111.

Child Poverty Action Group
Telephone: 0171 837 7979.

Kidscape
2 Grosvenor Gardens, London SW1W ODH
Kidscape will send you some excellent free booklets on keeping yourself safe. Send a large stamped self-addressed envelope. Phone: 0171 730 3300.

The Samaritans (24-hour)
Need someone to talk to? No problem is too big or too small. The Samaritans will talk to you in complete confidence. Or you can contact them by e-mail (they try to respond within 24 hours); look at their website on the Internet for information about them; or call in to a local office.
Lo-call: 0345 90 90 90.

Ireland: 1850 60 90.
E-mail: admin@samaritans.org.uk
Internet: http://www.samaritans.org.uk

USA   Boston: (617) 536-2460;
New York: (212) 753-0521.

HOMELESSNESS

UK   **Shelter**
National Campaign for Homeless People
Telephone: 0171-5052000.

IRRITABLE BOWEL SYNDROME

UK   **The IBS Network**
Northern General Hospital, Sheffield, S5 7AU.
Telephone: 01142-611531.

MENINGITIS

UK   **National Meningitis Trust**
Fern House, Bath Road, Stroud,
Gloucestershire, GL5 3TJ.
Telephone: 01453-751738
Helpline: (24 hours): 0845-6000800.

MISSING PERSONS

Message Home.
Left home? Send a message, no questions asked.
Freephone: 0800-700740.

NUTRITION

USA   **American Dietetic Association**
216 West Jackson Boulevard, Chicago, IL 60606.
Telephone: (800) 366-1655.

PERIOD PAIN AND PMT

UK **National Association for Pre-menstrual Syndrome**
PO Box 72, Sevenoaks, Kent TN13 1XQ.
Telephone: 01732-741709

National Endometriosis Society
50 Westminster Palace Gardens
1-7 Artillery Row, London, SW1P 1RL.
Telephone: 0171-2222776.

USA **National Women's Health Resource Center**
120 Albany Street, Suite 820
New Brunswick, NJ 08901.
Telephone: (732) 8288575.
Internet: http//www.healthy.women's.org/

RAPE and SEXUAL ABUSE

UK **Rape Crisis Centre**
Telephone: 0171-8371600.

USA **Rape Crisis (RAINN)**
Tollfree: 1800-656HOPE

SMOKING

UK **Smokers Quitline**
Freephone: 0800-002200.

USA **American Lung Association**
1740 Broadway, New York, NY 10019
Telephone: (212) 3158700.

FURTHER READING

Breast Health, Dr. Miriam Stoppard (Dorling Kindersley, 1998). *A clear and informative guide to everything a girl should know about breasts including how to do a self-examination..*

Cool & Celibate? Sex or No Sex, Dr. David Bull MB, BS, B.Sc., ASM (Element Children's Books, 1998).

The Element Family Encyclopedia of Health, Dr. R Sharma MB, Bch, LRCP & S(I), MRCH, MFHom (Element, 1998). A comprehensive guide to medical conditions including both complementary and orthodox medical treatments and prevention.

Mind Games, Mental Fitness for Tennis, J. & J. Whitmore (Element Children's Books, 1998). *An ace book with loads of great advice about how to win at whatever you want to do.*

Young Citizen's Passport, Your Guide To The Law, (Hodder & Stoughton, 1999)

The Vaccination Bible (What Doctors Don't Tell You, 1998) contains information on childhood, adult and travel vaccines. Available from WDDTY, 4 Wallace Road, London, N1 2PG.